THE DRIVEWAY DIARIES

THE DRIVEWAY

DIARIES

A DIRT ROAD ALMANAC

TIM BROOKES

TURTLE POINT PRESS NEW YORK

Copyright © 2005 by Turtle Point Press

LCCN 2004108024 ISBN 1-885586-33-7

Design and composition by Jeff Clark
at Wilsted & Taylor Publishing Services

Early versions of some of the stories in
The Driveway Diaries first appeared
in *Vermont Sunday Magazine, Vermont
Magazine,* and *U.S. Airways Attaché* and
were broadcast on National Public
Radio's "Sunday Weekend Edition"
and on North Country Public Radio.

Printed in Canada

CONTENTS

To Nick Meyer and Tom Blanchard

and everyone else who ever

mowed a neighbor's field or

ploughed a neighbor's driveway

INTRODUCTION

When we first moved to our modest house on a dirt road in Essex Center, Vermont, the only thing I noticed about the gravel driveway running down from the road to the side of the house was that it was a masterpiece of inconvenience, neither functional nor attractively rustic. A pain in the ass.

At the time, though, I was working on a doomed book about commuting, and spent far too much time thinking about driving, the land, and the vital importance of finding some sustainable relationship between the two before the car and its support systems—roads, for example—destroy everything we love about the land, and destroy us too. I started to develop an odd affection for dirt roads, poised between civilization and nature, sketching the perimeter of rational, suburban consciousness. The dirt road was the minimal impact, the lightest footprint—and my driveway was my own little dirt road.

I was also a new homeowner, and like every homeowner, I was dragged, kicking and cursing, to philosophy class by the sheer fact that everything we build, or plan, or intend, is subject to constant

1

decay and frequent catastrophe. A house is our place of safety and retreat, the place we furnish and decorate according to our sense of how the world should be. But a house is also a box wedged into the hillside, underground streams running downhill all around it, hydrostatic pressure pushing hard against the concrete of the foundation, ants wandering in under the porch door, mice running in the eaves, pollen drifting invisibly through the screens, the varnish on the front door blistering slowly in the summer sun. A wooden house is a slow shipwreck. So slow, in fact, that we barely notice the shifting of timbers, the curl of siding. But the driveway —the driveway was my blackboard. Constructed from natural materials, exposed to the elements, barely maintained—the driveway was right there in the disputed territory, the borderlands, showing every minuscule shift in the balance of power between order and chaos.

All these currents combined, or conspired, and I began to keep a driveway diary.

I'd spend the first couple of hours of the day in my basement office, working on my doomed book, staring at the computer, occasionally turning in my chair to gaze out of the window across the meadow and woodland in the valley. Around mid-morning, when I felt like a break, I walked up the driveway to get the mail. As soon as I stepped outdoors, everything changed. The air outside was different: fresh, complex. The temperature was different, too—warmer or colder than indoors, it actually felt like a temperature, rather than just a climate. Most of all, though, the light was powerful, authentic. I'd squint and look down as I headed up toward the road, and what I saw under the benediction of this glorious half-blindness was the driveway and the land on both sides of it, which seemed to be bursting out of the ground like a revelation.

The smallest things were irradiated with significance: a grasshopper flicking off to one side; a chip of quartz, glinting; the half-dead potentilla bush throwing out a tiny exclamation of leaves on apparently barren twig; the telephone purr of crickets; the ridge at the top of the driveway where the gravel road had been regraded so often it was now an inch and a half lower than the apron at the head of the driveway.

At the same time, I began to notice how often driveways turned up in other Vermonters' conversations, especially in times of trouble. In winter, driveway health maintenance was a thriving blue-collar industry, and anyone who owned a pickup and a Fisher plow blade was everyone's best friend. Whenever there was an ice storm, people would be absent at work and show up the following day shrugging, saying "I just couldn't get out of my driveway."

The rural driveway, then, is a kind of vital umbilicus between the safety of home and the activity of the outside world, a stalk between the trunk of the road and the apple of the house. Of all the accidents and misguided acts of folly that taught me about life in Vermont, the driveway taught me the most.

3

Oh, one final word. These are the elements. Composition: mostly gravel, some soil, miscellaneous weeds. Average width, nine feet. Length, thirty yards, maybe a little more. Rises a good fifteen feet, from the flat apron in front of the garage door past the foot of the front steps to the sharp little lip just before the landing at the top, by the road. Steep, in other words. Deceptively steep.

YEAR ONE

SEE THE LAND

In early April, when Vermont was still soggy and flattened by the retreating winter, my best friend Vince Feeney, a historian who became a realtor just for a good excuse to poke around in old houses, drove me out along Route 15 to Essex Center, the word "center" in Vermont meaning "middle of nowhere." He turned off the main road at the old brick hall where the local theater group puts on its plays, passed the pulpwood dealer with its line of trailers full of logs, and branched up a road that offered fewer and fewer houses and seemed to be heading in the general direction of Canada. Within half a mile the paved road became a dirt road. Vince bumped past a sizeable apple orchard and an abandoned wooden silo, and as the vegetation on each side was becoming increasingly ragged he finally pulled up at the head of a gravel driveway.

The house lay down below the height of the road, small, undistinguished, rather ugly, its siding painted Vermont barn-red, its trim a rather weathered white. Vince parked in a small bay or landing by the road and led the way down the driveway, which ran rather steeply down to the left of the house, past a handmade set

7

of wooden steps that ran up to a front door, its varnish peeling in the sunlight. Inside the front door, the stairs inside went either down or up—we were coming into a split-level ranch at the split, it seemed—and he went up. This was the kitchen-dining-living-room, with hardwood floors and a high ceiling, and above all it was full of light. The light flooded in through sliding French glass doors that opened onto a second-floor deck, and the deck over-looked the land.

The view lay westward, and as all hills and valleys in Vermont run north-south, the view took in a small yard area at the foot of the deck, an apron of lawn bordered by spruce trees, then a strip of wild meadowland running left and right, and beyond the meadow, perhaps 200 yards away, a mixed woodland of pine, spruce, maple, birch, and a dozen other kinds of tree, also running up and down the valley. Beyond that, all I could see was a couple of houses on the road that ran up the far side of the valley, perhaps a mile away, and above them a low range of wooded hills. Ten acres of this, Vince said, arranged in a lot that ran roughly in the shape of a strip of lasagna back to the brook at the heart of the val-ley, came with the house.

Ten acres. In England, where I was born and lived for the first half of my life, you can't have ten acres unless you are an Earl, or are sleeping with an Earl, or are the outcome of someone else sleeping with an Earl. I barely looked at the house. I looked at the

8

land and saw everything my mother had ever planted in a garden, plus everything that she had always wanted to plant in a garden, but had never had garden enough. I saw blueberry bushes, apple trees, blackberry bushes, grapevines, and a rototilled vegetable garden so large I could plant corn, a vegetable that would be inconceivable in tiny English gardens, as it would block the neighbor's sunlight.

I even saw things that only Earls have in gardens. There was a damp spot some sixty yards from the house that I imagined getting someone over to backhoe and making a pond. (This despite the fact that I know nobody who backhoes. I'm not sure I'm even spelling it correctly. The Earl would, of course, have several foresters and gardeners who knew about ponds and backhoes and such rustic stuff.) And beside the pond, Japanese maples and a weeping willow. And beyond the pond, in the rest of the meadow before the tree line, there was almost room for a cricket field. . . .

In short, I thought (apart from the cricket field) like an American. Americans don't realize how avid and how fundamental to their identity the desire to own land has always been. As soon as I landed on these shores I was struck by the way in which an American homeowner, gesturing out of the back windows, would refer not to his garden or his yard but to his *property*, as if ownership were more important than the thing being owned—which in many cases, of course, it was.

Blind to what was actually there, I saw what ought to be there. The unimaginable vastness of the property struck me, as the great plains must have struck the early pioneers, as a kind of all-you-can-eat buffet—another American notion, unimaginable in England. Anything was possible—and with an equally American combination of boundless energy, limitless ambition, and almost complete ignorance, I would make this vast plot of land into everything that it was not, and everything that England was not.

Vince and I drove back into Burlington, a city of potted ferns, a city that has at best a nodding acquaintance with the rest of Vermont, and told Barbara that I'd found our house.

"Well?" she asked eagerly. "What's it like?"

"Frankly, the house isn't much," I admitted. "But the land," I went on, gazing away over her shoulder, my eyes adjusting to focus just beyond the horizon. "You should see the land. You should see the potential."

DROUGHT BUFFALO

These are the thoughts of a first-time homeowner-to-be, ninety minutes before closing on his dream house.

You know the place. This is the unassuming little house that gains its splendor and color from its surroundings: the lilac tree up by the road, the assortment of interesting (if nameless) little shrubs and bushes running around the skirts of the house, the morning glories climbing up and disguising the ugly cinder-block chimney, the day-lilies and daffodils running away down the slope of the property line . . .

. . . and, round the back, the blueberry bushes he has already bought and the apple trees he plans to, the huge garden that is already being rototilled as part of the purchase agreement, the grapevine he plans to get to trail over the fence, and, beyond it all, the long meadow with its soft ankle-deep grass that he plans to bisect with a graceful, curving mown path, sprinkled and bordered with wildflowers whose names he also does not yet know, but surely the Vermont Wildflower Farm on Route 7 can fill him in on the technical stuff.

At least, that was to have been the house. It still was the house of his mind's eye until about eleven this morning, when he and his friendly realtor, Vince, went out to do one last walk-through of the property before the closing.

He had not paid a lot of attention, frankly, to the news that Vermont was rapidly becoming a drought state. Yes, he had noticed that the lawn of the house in Burlington that he was currently renting had turned brown and shriveled up, but that simply meant he didn't have to mow it in addition to all the other ten thousand preparations for moving, which was, in fact, a blessing. And being still on town water he had no hesitation in watering his own potted plants (including the blueberry bushes) and the neat little flower beds of the rented house in question.

Outside Burlington, it quickly became apparent that drought, like serious snow, begins outside the city limits. The dream house is out in rural Essex, near the Westford line, and at first sight it doesn't look too desperate. Admittedly, the lawn resembles light brown Astroturf, but lawns are expected to be casualties of dry summers, right?

On closer inspection, all the interesting (if nameless) little bushes and shrubs skirting the house are now slightly less interesting collections of twigs, with an occasional leathery leaf clinging to a twig like an overcooked nacho chip. Not to worry, the homeowner-to-be says to himself, this is where the new blueberry bushes will go. Now how about the apple trees?

Surveying the front of the house, his heart suddenly sinks. Surely that thing there actually is an apple tree, or was: this mature growth, fully ten feet tall, has barely a leaf left. What chance will his own adolescent trees have, still suffering from the shock of being uprooted and tied to the roof of an aging Volvo?

The back of the house shows the true extent of the disaster. The flower beds are a thicket of weeds that have leaped up a good four feet while the more delicate flowers between them were staggering and choking. The patches of bare earth here and there are the texture of ground fiberglass. He tries to imagine planting a vegetable garden in this stuff and watering it three times a day....

This is the final nightmare. He is no longer on town water. He stops, stunned, realizing at last what a complete Eddie Albert he has been, moving to his Green Acres with so little rural knowledge that he can't tell the difference between a well and a wallflower. He is no longer on town water. If he tries to plant now, with the aquifer level falling like a stone, every watering will be at the expense of the drinking water, every shower will come out of his blueberries. Essex Center is now starting to feel like Amarillo, only with a higher pollen count.

On the drive back to Burlington, City of a Thousand Sprinklers, he hears that one Vermont town has already been declared a drought disaster, and that the National Guard has dispatched a buffalo, apparently some kind of mobile tanker, to help out the parched townspeople, clutching at the guardsmen's camouflaged

13

sleeves like Somalis. And that all kinds of small insects, their hour come round at last, are taking advantage of the plants' weakened defenses and attacking in droves. Swarms.

"Have you noticed any signs that the well is running low?" he asks the sellers, desperately, at the closing.

"Well, we haven't started drinking silt yet," they say, and chuckle.

He reaches for his checkbook with a sense of doom, as if to buy Tom Joad's house in dust-bowl Oklahoma.

14

LAWNMOWER MAN

The lawnmower man lived in a town that for anonymity's sake I'll call Milford, which could therefore be Milton or Westford or somewhere whose name is completely different, like Bennington. When I called the number he listed in the *Buyer's Digest*, he gave me directions to find a certain trailer park, which, like all trailer parks, had been given the kind of name the British landed gentry gave their 5,000-acre feudal estates. I should take the second entrance to the trailer park and follow the road as it snaked this way and that until it finally reached a dead end, and then count back five trailers on the right.

The trailer park was actually rather nice. Coleridge says of Xanadu, the palace of Kublai Khan, that "There were forests, ancient as the hills, / Enfolding sunny spots of greenery," and it must be said that this trailer park was surrounded by forest and had sunny spots of greenery among the trailers.

The fifth trailer from the dead end came with a small patch of property surrounded by a chain-link fence, which enclosed not only the trailer itself but several small sheds, each overflowing with small mechanical carcasses: mowers, mopeds, snowblowers, chainsaws, outboard motors. Beside the trailer stood a large Yamaha motorbike with a torn seat, and an orphan Honda lay on the grass beside it with the forlorn look of a helpless piece of equipment about to be cannibalized.

The lawnmower man was tuning the engine of a stripped-down mini-bike when I strolled over and called his name.

He was a tall, handsome man in his thirties, I'd say, with thinning dark hair and a grin that came and went too easily, as if he oiled that, too, on a regular basis. He looked me up and down. His tan, from hours spent wrestling in the back yard with small carburetors and tiny throttle cables, was deeper than mine, but in my sandals, shorts, and T-shirt I was clearly out of place, a man of wealth and leisure among the working poor. I reminded him I'd called the previous night about used lawnmowers. He looked at me askance—that is, sideways and cunningly.

"Who do you work for?" he demanded.

Startled, I reassured him that I had no connection with any lawnmower dealers or with the I.R.S., and one of these answers seemed to satisfy him, for he went over to one of his small sheds and hauled out one of the Lawn Chiefs that had been abandoned under heavy shellfire by the retreating Republican Guard somewhere north of Kuwait. The motor started gamely enough,

16

though, and he moved it a couple of feet back and forth to show that it came complete with a cutting blade.

"That one's fifty-five," he said, "But I'll let you have it for fifty." He checked my expression quickly for signs of trouble, and he laughed extravagantly at his own jokes.

I enquired whether he had any other mowers for sale. Well, yes, as it happened: he also had this Lawn Boy.

"What shape is that one in?" I asked.

"Lawn Boy's a Lawn Boy," he said cryptically, as he pulled it out of the shed, and while I was trying to work out whether he was apologizing or boasting, he gave it a slug of gas and the Lawn Boy, too, chugged back and forth, shaving another half-inch off the sandy grass.

In fact, when I pressed him it transpired that all the mowers in the last shed were for sale; there was clearly some cunning to his sales pitch that I was missing. The largest and newest was a red creature with a large Briggs and Stratton engine.

"Course, if you're interested in looks . . ." he said, as if trying to discourage me. Again, I wasn't sure what was going on. Of course I wasn't interested in looks, I said, but of course I was: I wanted something that looked as if it would survive another few months' hard labor among the weeds, and whose parts all seemed to have been made at the same time by the same manufacturer. The Briggs and Stratton started easily and ran with a low purr.

17

I asked if it came with a bagger. He looked around and seized a dusty, crumpled bagger from a shelf. This was it, he said. I was in luck. He began turning it inside out and knocking the sands of Araby off it. I pointed out that the bagger, while being of about the right size, clearly didn't fit any of the appropriate attachments and prongs on the back of the mower, and after a couple of minutes' fiddling and wrenching he conceded I was right. Anyway, a grass bag, he said, would be more bother than it was worth. I'd be emptying it every couple of passes. It wasn't until I got it home that I saw the large sign warning me never to operate this machine without a grass bag.

The Briggs would be $55, he said, $50 for cash. The Lawn Boy was $45, and the poor Lawn Chief had now fallen to $40. I bought the Briggs, and he gave me some earnest advice on draining the oil and helped me load it into my trunk.

In a sense, I was set up to be a sucker—after all, he could tell me almost anything about his mowers and even if I didn't actually believe him, I couldn't prove him wrong. But if he had information and guile on his side, I had a luxury he didn't have, and might never have: I could afford to be ripped off.

In effect, I was buying a fifty-five-dollar adventure among the working poor, and if I was lucky I might get a working lawnmower thrown into the bargain. If the machine held up long enough to cut the lawn, say, twice before the end of the summer, I could con-

18

sider it money well spent, and if not, it would make a good story. Who was manipulating whom?

We shook hands, he gave his sly grin again, and I left him in his trailer park. And when I wedged open the bagger door, using a paint stirrer, the Briggs sprayed my left calf with sharp fragments of grass and twig, but otherwise it worked just fine.

WASP VIETNAM

One of the first jobs I tackled after we had bought our house was to paint the outside of the building, and the first of many obstacles that made the painting drag on for month after month was the wasps.

After several days of swiping at them with the roller and spraying myself with little cream-colored commas of Sherwin-Williams #2446 Eidelweiss, I called in Grenier's Pest Control. I showed Paul Grenier, Jr., two holes in the siding where I'd seen wasps crawling in and out, and he duly puffed a little powder in each and taped over the holes. The whole process took ten minutes. He generously reduced his bill, seeing as he hadn't had to wear his bee suit on a day that had long passed ninety degrees, but I still felt a little foolish.

The next day I took the ladder round to the front of the house, and as I propped it against the eaves I noticed that since I had last looked at that side, the building had grown an excrescence, a bulbous gray papery mass the size of a melon with a spiral design running round it and a black hole at the bottom . . . and as my mind was trying to produce something sensible in the way of output, a wasp crawled out of the hole and flew off.

"Those are hornets," my wife said, looking worried. She wanted to have Grenier come back in his bee suit and take the nest down while we were sheltering in a different zip code, but I wouldn't listen. It would cost $75, but more importantly, I said, trotting out one of those gems of philosophy that are guaranteed to get you into trouble, *we would never learn anything by having others run our risks for us.* Besides, they looked more like ordinary yellow-jacket wasps to me. Admittedly, I'd never seen a hornet, but Barbara was from New Jersey, and I wouldn't trust her to know a hornet from a hamster.

I wasn't exactly sure how to deal with a wasp's nest. Grenier had mentioned a spray. The lawnmower man, I remembered, had used a cheaper method. "I had three of 'em on my trailer," he said, gesturing wildly, "so I just took a broom and went 'Bam! Bam! Bam!'"

Paul Meehan, of Meehan's Tree Service, stopping by to look at our impacted spruce trees, had a great deal more respect for nests.

"Those are white-faced wasps," he said, peering up at the eaves in alarm. "They'll chase you right down the road." Best thing to do, he said, was to wait until evening or early morning, when the wasps are sluggish (an interesting notion: is there also a time when slugs are waspish?), creep up a ladder with an empty paint can, slam it over the nest, and slide something flat between the can and the eaves, trapping the brutes. Once he had come across an active nest as big as a medicine ball on a branch twenty feet up. His men maneuvered an oil drum into position, he snipped through the branch, the nest fell neatly into the can, and his men quickly tossed in an insecticide bomb and slammed the lid. Mind you, he said, if his aim had been a foot off. . .and we both silently imagined the nest being sliced open by the rim of the drum, the insects boiling out.

If these genuine Vermonters could use such primitive, even daft methods, spraying seemed a pretty safe option. I bought The Enforcer Foam! Kills Wasps, Hornets and Yellow Jackets with a 20 Ft Blast! Mind you, even The Enforcer Foam! stressed the danger of the operation: as soon as I'd finished spraying, the can said, I should leave the area immediately. This was fine by me, but how far? The end of the road? Switzerland?

And when should I attack? Evening was out, as I would be spraying toxic chemicals right outside Maddy's bedroom window, and at five months old Maddy was probably as vulnerable to this spray as the wasps were. It would have to be early morning—and in a desperate attempt to make my suicide mission seem routine, even jaunty, I proposed that we hit the nest, leap into the car, and go out for breakfast.

Next day, we overslept. Two days later we were struggling out of bed at 6 a.m. Having no bee suit, I decided to pad myself as thickly as possible: shorts, jeans, another pair of pants (tucked into my work boots), T-shirt, sweater, down jacket with hood, wool hat. . . . Barbara found an industrial face mask and insisted that it would protect my asthmatic lungs from the fumes. When I put it on, my glasses fogged up. I threw it away.

By the time she had dressed Maddy and both of them were safely in the car with the windows rolled up and the engine running, it was 6:40. What time did wasps get up? Had they already left the nest?

As I climbed the ladder, a strange kind of remorse was creeping over me. On the radio I had heard an interview with a Buddhist monk who once shared his house with bees that crawled all over him. After all, he said calmly, the bees lived here first. When I thought about it, getting stung was not such a big deal. The wasps only had stings; I had tetramethrin and 3-phenoxybenzyl cyclopropanecarboxylate. I thought of Vietnam, and I pressed the button.

A stream of liquid foam leaped from the nozzle and coated the mouth of the nest, building up and dripping off. I kept spraying, certain that if the stream wavered for an instant from the mouth of the nest, a phalanx of wasps would struggle through the foam, burst out en masse, and swarm down at me in their fury.

After a few seconds, the entire nest began to look soft and soggy.

23

No swarm. In a surprisingly short time the spray ran out. The nest looked like a small gray sponge that had been hit with a foam fire extinguisher.

I scrambled down the ladder, threw the can aside, got into the car, and watched. Several dead or dying wasps fell out of the dripping nest.

A moment later, a lone wasp appeared from above the roof. We were too late. We had not got them all. It circled the dead structure, and I thought of Germans returning to Hamburg after World War II, wandering through the rubble in search of their families, and what had once been their home.

I headed off to breakfast, stung by the fact that once again fear had made a fool of me.

STAMPING
HYSTERICALLY

When I was painting the house, using a ladder I borrowed from Vince, I heard a burring sound by my ear and froze, thinking it was an enormous wasp or bee, a species that grew so large only out here in the country, possibly the great-grandsire of the wasps I had exterminated, who had emerged from a nest the size of a termite mound to avenge his little offspring. I slowly moved my paintbrush hand down to the ladder to brace myself, then carefully turned my head. It was a hummingbird. I didn't even know hummingbirds summered this far north.

Several times when I was at the top of the ladder, leaning forward and ducking to get under the eaves, I had to clear out extensive spiderwebs, one of which was inhabited by a spider so big I nearly fell off the ladder. I could barely bring myself to look at it. Yet at the same time as I was still thrumming with aftershocks, trying to work up the nerve to wreck the web with my paint stick, it struck me that first, the spider wasn't *that* big—no bigger than, say, a brown apricot—and second, that this wasp/spider/humming-bird/whatever terror had something to do with trespass.

This was not my territory. I didn't know the inhabitants, or the rules—I didn't *belong* here. And as soon as that feeling takes good root, almost anything, even a hummingbird, can be a threat, and I want to react hysterically, to stamp it out.

What a particularly American experience this must be. The early colonists' fear of the wilderness, the unknown, and their hysterical desire to stamp out the inhabitants, for whom this was home.

WHALES OF
THE LAND

Soon after I bought the house, I did something I'd never done before, and had never thought of doing: I had three trees cut down.

I still couldn't believe I owned ten acres, but somehow the ten acres were more of a liability than an asset. As half our land was wetland and half was wooded, it would have cost far more to develop than it was worth. Consequently, its cost was invisible: we bought the entire property for $115,000, which was the price of the house, but then found ourselves looking at a $3,000 tax bill for the land. I could barely bring order to the flower beds, let alone the other 9.95 acres. In a way, it was a trap: like many other people along our road, I became the steward of far more of the valley than I could conscientiously manage.

The trees were the first victims of my lordly illusions. Our . . . um . . . property came with perhaps a couple of thousand trees, fifty or more lining the road, a dozen marking the southern property line, a hundred in a dense windbreak to the north of the house, and the rest in a thick tree line, three hundred yards away, of which we owned a section. The first time I explored this little forest, I couldn't grasp that this was mine. In England, I'd always thought of trees as a kind of public property, as if the National Trust owned everything that was green and more than six feet tall. I didn't know anyone with more than a quarter-acre of land, and I didn't know anyone who owned a chainsaw.

So I was astonished when Vince recommended that we cut down two ash trees that obscured a little of the magnificent view of the valley, and equally aghast when a landscape designer airily talked of clearing out this and taking out that, as if land were like Legos, and it was simply a matter of getting down to bedrock and starting afresh with the right pieces. Instead, I found myself thinking that trees were more like whales — large, placid, uncomplaining beings, fortunate while they were irrelevant to us, in danger as soon as we deemed them useful and turned on them our busy, extractive inventiveness.

In a broader sense, I also found myself worrying about the whole question of "improvement." I wanted to make the place more beautiful, but what right did I have to determine what was beautiful — especially if my choices meant that what I found beautiful would live, and anything else would die?

As soon as I began painting the house, things started to go badly for the trees. Some previous owner had, insanely, planted a pine

28

tree two feet from the house, between the driveway and the south wall of the garage. By now it was sixteen feet tall. It prevented our cars from getting into the garage, and I couldn't paint behind it without being ripped to shreds by its needles. A tree surgeon stopped by, pointed out that the pine roots would damage my foundations, and offered to remove it and two charmless, half-dead spruce that were stealing all the light from one end of the flower beds. "Do it," I said, trying to sound as if I shredded trees every day. A hundred bucks converted all three to wood chips, which I didn't know how to use. In the same campaign I also went after a gnarled and spiteful juniper hedge that had grown six feet up one wall and then dried into vicious little thorns. I regarded the juniper in much the same light as the wasps—after all, I had Zoë and Maddy to protect—and painfully cut it down to ground level.

Now I had a painted house and a quasi-functioning driveway, but I was a wreck. What should I do about all this land, these trees, even these weeds? How would I best take care of what was now legally mine, over which I'd been given the power, literally, of life and death? Writing in *The New Yorker*, Jamaica Kincaid said that when a landscaper advised her to remove the trees around her house in southern Vermont, she waited until he left and then went around apologizing to the trees.

Perhaps I should plant a tree for every one I had cut down; but planting trees in itself does them no favors, either. The Scotch

29

pines planted at the northern end of the house as a windbreak were put in too close together, too close to the house and too close to a trio of pear trees. The pears, linking and locking branches with the nearest evergreens, were choked and unhealthy, and one spruce was given so little space in one angle of the house that it was forced back on itself until its branches were knitted in among each other like the tentacles of an anxious octopus.

So I was a sucker for the mailing from the National Arbor Day Foundation that asked me for ten bucks and promised me six blue spruce as a signing-on gift. I planted the spruce in August. By spring they were still only a foot tall, and by summer they had vanished in the weeds, which I daren't cut for fear of decapitating my sole contributions to the reforestation of Vermont.

I found myself standing at the foot of the driveway, staring at the clean, bright stump of the felled spruce. There was no getting away from it: there's no National Trust here, and this land, these trees, were entrusted to me, God help them.

THE LAST OF THE
SUMMER VINES

A good garden season leaves you with little to say, only with tomatoes to can and zucchini to give away.

A bad summer leaves you overflowing with a different and more
bitter fruit, which you also want to give away to anyone who will
take it: complaints about the deer or the Japanese beetle, tales of
wells gone dry or hail a day before harvest.

This year was a good year for bad garden stories. My own began
right after we moved, when I began planting, already a month late
and in the face of the state's worst drought on record. The soil was
untended and unfertilized, except where the previous owners had
penned their eighteen sled dogs—and in those areas I kept coming across large concrete lumps that were the feet of fence posts.
Still, I raised mounds and beds and threw in an assortment of
the usual seeds, studiously ignoring the plant-by dates on the packets. At the local farm store, already marking down its seedlings, I
bought tomato plants like skinny orphans, each one a thin, weak

stem four inches high with a pair of flaccid yellowish leaves clinging to the tip. A sprinkler would have flattened them; we had to
trickle water from a cupped hand around their wispy roots, like
feeding nestlings with a dropper bottle.

We had little enough water anyway: it was our first year on a
well, and there was no knowing how long it would last. Week in
and week out, the well-drillers' truck appeared in one neighbor's
driveway after another up and down the valley, and another poor
soul found himself with a deeper well and a bill for $4,000.
Whenever the bathwater wasn't too soapy, I'd scoop a gallon or so
in the watering-can that stood beside the shampoo and the yellow
plastic duck and go out to revive another small patch of parched
soil.

The torrential rains that left half the state flooded must have arrived at a crucial point in the garden's growth curve, for within a
week the earth exploded. The tomatoes, suddenly free of wilt, became thick, dark bushes, merging first with their neighbors and
then leaping across from one row to the next to meet one of the
other varieties coming in the opposite direction, or leaning heavily over the luxuriant but shorter pepper plants like playground
bullies, filching their sun.

In August, the storm that blew down half of the Adirondack National Forest roared across the valley and toppled everything sideways. The tomato cages were bent almost at right angles where

they went into the ground; the pea-and-bean trellis, sheltered by the rest of the garden, abandoned the vertical and began leaning drunkenly on its own vegetation.

Before we could fix any of this, we had to go away for six days, and by the time we came back open warfare had broken out. The tomatoes were now a solid hedge five feet tall, under which the peppers, beets, and bok choy in the next row had vanished. The pumpkins, cucumbers, and squash on the other side had punched through the tomato hedge to reappear three rows away, throwing up their huge, insolent yellow flowers like mouths braying in triumph.

The garden had become a parable of unrestrained development. "Growth! Growth!" the squash family was yelling, galloping in like a pack of out-of-state developers and trampling everything under its vines, while the foolish lettuce, still crying "Local control! Local control!" was choked and flattened.

Yet in this thicket of fecundity, something was clearly wrong; we had missed some crucial deadline. We got some twenty smallish zucchini, but our thousand or more tomatoes refused to ripen. The peas flowered and flowered but never podded, and the half-dozen pepper plants, barely visible under the tomato jungle, produced a single pepper the size of an acorn.

Only the green beans stuck to their task, and at the last possible moment, three days before the first frost, hundreds of tiny beans appeared, like green icicles. We ate them off the stem, recognizing that this was Nature's token gratitude that we had never, in spite of everything, abandoned the garden.

The first frost came early and hard. First all the pumpkin leaves blackened and drooped, and the basil, cucumber, and zucchini; then another frost, and another. The tomatoes wilted, their hard green fruit untouched and emerging like false pearls, and the peas and beans looked scarred.

Yet, peering closer, I found that the beans under the broadest leaves had been sheltered, and had been growing with the same desperate enthusiasm that all the vegetables had been showing all summer. Many were now more than six inches long. We picked three dozen or so, steamed them, and ate them that night as yet another frost stalked in, and a million stars punctuated the dark universe.

THE REVENGE OF
THE DRIVEWAY

If I thought about the driveway at all, in the first few weeks after we moved in, I thought it was scruffy. The gravel was threadbare, with weeds and earth showing through. Its borders were ill-defined, its depth uneven — it was an affront to my English sense of good housekeeping, and one of my first projects was to take the driveway in hand. It would be six months before I realized that the driveway was a trap, a kind of Advanced Vermont Living Test, and I would fail it.

In the balmy days of summer I ordered a couple of dozen railroad ties from a man called Noel Viens, who in his spare time sold Catholic life insurance, or perhaps it was the other way round. The first sign that things were going wrong was a strange noise we heard coming from the neighbors' front yard, a kind of whining and crashing. Shortly afterwards, there was a knock on the front door, and my insurance-and-railroad friend told me rather sheepishly that they'd delivered the ties to the wrong house. Once he had scooped them all up again with the cherry-picker and dumped them in our front yard, and I saw the enormous gouges that the pulpwood truck had left in the soft ground on each side of our driveway, I cringed at the thought of what my neighbor would think when he got home.

Over the next few days I edged the driveway with several of the ties, which weighed approximately the same as lead and could only be moved by rolling, thus flattening anything growing in their path. After about forty-five minutes of this work, I had to stop and have a little lie down, massaging my lower back. Still, the drive now looked much neater, and I even persuaded some bird's-foot trefoil to grow over one of the ties.

The story now takes a break of three or four months, during which the driveway looks both neat and attractively rustic, and I unwittingly look like an idiot.

Amazingly, it wasn't until the first snow that I realized how steep the driveway actually was. My car, a ten-year-old Volvo, had no chance of making it, and I took to parking it in the little bay thoughtfully stationed at the top of the drive next to the road. Barbara's Toyota, with its front wheel drive, had an outside chance of making it up and down, and morning after morning we both shoveled, me still limping and hopping from the knee surgery I'd undergone in late fall. Then she took between five and fifteen runs backwards, each time getting a little closer to that accursed crest,

36

clawing on the brink with her engine screaming at 7000 rpm, her snow tires rapidly changing into summer tires, before she slid back down to the front door again or, if she wasn't careful, into the lilac tree. When she did finally make it over the crest, smashing backwards through the snowbank left by the plough, she was going so fast that if the school bus were coming along at that moment. . . . I didn't want to think about it.

"Weren't you going to call someone about ploughing the driveway?" she demanded a little caustically. I had actually called our neighbor, who like 44 percent of all neighbors in Essex Center has a pickup with a plough blade, but he was booked up. Besides which, one morning the representative of Cota Landscaping, who had been ploughing the majestic, asphalted drive that led up to the palatial house opposite ours, paused to see if, in a neighborly way, he could help me out. He stared down our driveway while I rested on my snow shovel, panting and clutching my knee.

"I'd help you out," he said kindly, "but you ent got no laaandin'."

He was right: I had no landing—that is, there was nowhere to plough the snow *to*. He needed to shove it off the driveway, and I'd made a driveway with no off, thanks to my artistic wooden edging, now hidden under three feet of snow and ice. I had been thinking about Vermont like an outsider, and the driveway had struck back.

OFF-STREET PARKING

We try to make the best of it, leaving a sled at the head of the driveway, stacking the grocery bags in it and sledding them down to the front door, but there's no denying it: having to park at the head of the driveway all winter is a major pain.

This is how it works. Whoever gets home first pulls into the bay at the head of the driveway as far as possible, preferably ramming firmly into the snowbank at the end. The second car home pulls in as snugly as possible behind the first, thus ending up sideways across the head of the driveway.

For the car farther into the bay, the problems are pretty simple: you get snowed on and plowed in, and it can take a good half hour to dig yourself out. Also, because the ground in the bay tends to get compressed in the same spots time after time, the bay is somewhat icier, and in the morning you may need to throw down salt, cat litter, carpet squares, newspaper, or anything else handy in order to get a grip. You may have to dig, or scoop, or shovel, or chip away at the ice in order to get out—but that's still the cushy spot. It's the car behind it, the one that pulls in across the head of the driveway, that faces the real difficulties.

If you pull in too snugly, everything goes well until next morning, when you try to reverse out. If you don't cut the wheel enough to the right, you back straight into the snowbank under Zoë's tree house. If you then run forward and cut the wheel too hard, the front end—the end with the engine, the heavy end—swings left over the steepest part of the driveway, and if there's enough ice (and after you've backed into the snowbank a couple of times, you've *made* enough ice) the front starts to slide down the driveway, pulling the rest of the car after it. Then you're really in trouble.

If you don't pull in snugly enough, though, the rear of the car might stick out maybe six inches over the road proper. Then, at four in the morning, the phone rings. You grope for it. "Is this Mr. Brookes? This is the Essex police. The snowplow driver reports that your car's on the street. Go out and move it." Nothing apologetic in that tone at all. Get up, get dressed, move it, and move it *now*.

YEAR TWO

THE MOVEMENT
OF BIRDS

Last Thanksgiving we perched the camera on the frozen birdbath, ran to take up positions, and photographed ourselves in our snowsuits, squatting in eighteen inches of snow out the back of the house. A week ago—that is, four months later—there was still eighteen inches of snow there, and it was hard not to think that the same damned stuff had been there for more than a third of a year. A third of a year! And this is supposedly a mild winter! It hardly bears thinking about.

Then we had two warm days, and overnight the birds arrived.

There is no sound without movement, and in winter, most of the time, there is neither sound nor movement, but now the garden is full of both.

I'd forgotten how iridescent grackles are, green and black and blue at once, like African starlings, and how odd and penetrating their round yellow eyes look, and how they gather in gangs to populate one tree, then collectively rush off to another, and how they can spend the entire morning stitching back and forth between the trees at each side of our property.

The red-winged blackbirds have arrived too, looking for uprights to master and spy from, swaying steadily in the slight breeze. The hawk crosses the meadow in two wingbeats, pulls up at the tree line a hundred and fifty yards away, and perches in a tree so dead I can't even see it. He seems to be resting in midair.

The bluejays, who had the place to themselves for so long, chirp their one-two, one-two food call over and over, even though I haven't filled the bird feeder since early March. Two fat mourning doves are sitting on the rail by the steps leading down to the garden.

Even the flies have appeared instantaneously, looking suspiciously large and mating at once along the rail of the porch. At Chapin Orchard down the road, the first two lambs arrived two days ago, and now I come to think of it, this is the Easter weekend, and resurrection is taking place everywhere. Even the frozen ground is opening, like the rock at the mouth of the cave, and hydrostatic pressure is forcing up little springs everywhere. The back lawn — or rather the flattened brown tussocks that are the once and future lawn — is speckled with brown patches like large worm casts, where the underground streamlets are forced up so hard that we can hear them leaping an inch or two out of the ground. They bring particles of soil with them, which tail away downhill in small parallel smears.

44

Birds call from every direction; it's as though noise itself, frozen all winter, has thawed, and the silence of the snow is being swept away. The foot-wide culvert that runs under the dirt road is rushing with meltwater that disappears immediately under the remaining icy crust. I can hear it, but I can't see it. No, here it is, reappearing down under the bushes, carving a substantial little channel for itself past the bluebird houses. After lunch, a light rain drums onto the small porch roof, beats along the walkway at the side of the garage, drips heavily into the puddle forming outside my office window.

Smell has thawed, too, with the overwhelming smell of dogshit everywhere—who ever thought there were that many dogs around here?—and the windows, now open, let it all in.

Winter also enforces a moral freeze, a moratorium on things that should be done but now simply can't be done, and all those neglected tasks are now back to chide me: the half-assed spring cleaning I did a month ago left an armchair, some recycling, the garden hose, the late hamster's wheel, and two small cotton rugs folded right outside the garage door, where they were immediately buried. Now they're back, sodden and useless, and I'll have to do something about them at last, along with the scraps of wood I stacked to make a toy-chest for Maddy. The stuff is probably no good now, but I'd better check.

Yes, it's a trudging time, a discovering and doing time, a time when the yuppie hiking boots I managed to finagle for free are no good, and the old leather clod-hoppers come out so I can splash through standing water and mud, when the earth slowly opens up to let us sink into it. My God: there's a steady stream of meltwater running *out of the side of the road itself.*

A small avalanche of snow just rumbled off the roof. Yes! This is the value of suffering.

HOUSEHOLD
OF ITCHES

In the last few weeks we've been thinking a lot about the people from whom we bought the house, who sold up fast and moved to Alaska, leaving no forwarding address. No, seriously: they wanted to race sled dogs, and Vermont just wasn't cold enough for them. I've also been learning a lot about water.

As soon as we moved in, the septic system collapsed. This was an educational experience, as I hung out with the guy from P&P Septic and learned that after a couple of days with your trench exposed to the open air and the contents oxidizing, it doesn't smell nearly as bad. "I don't barely notice it, half the time," he said.

Then Barbara discovered that there was a strange gray rectangle on the ceiling of the refrigerator that looked oddly like duct tape. On closer inspection, we found that it half-covered some kind of leak, and the inside of the fridge was subject to a slow, cold rain, as condensation formed constantly and dripped onto everything beneath. It's amazing how unappetizing a fresh apple pie looks when covered with blood runoff from the packet of beef on the shelf above.

The fridge had to go, as did the dishwasher, which instead of cleaning the dishes removed all the particles of food and then generously redistributed them all over everything and then baked them on hard, creating an effect that artists call pointillism. Especially distressing whenever Barbara decided to wash the empty cat-food cans. Then the washing machine gave up the ghost like a noble Roman after what the appliance repair guy estimated as several decades at its post.

But appliances are appliances the world over. What I wasn't ready for was the holding tank.

The holding tank was a fat gray cylinder under the stairs; some kind of pipe ran into it under the driveway from the well. In England, people don't have wells, they have municipal water boards. When I told my brother, who has rebuilt several houses, that we were on a well, a silence came over the phone, and he repeated "A well?" as if such devices were still used only in Jordan, or Romania.

From what I could gather, the holding tank had a vestibular function: it allowed the water to come in from the great outdoors and pause to knock the mud off its molecules, so to speak, before entering the house proper and mingling with the plumbing. It also had something to do with maintaining a constant pressure, at

48

which it was not very good. Water issued from the taps and the shower in great long sine waves, ebbing to almost nothing and then flowing back up to spring tide proportions, rising and falling as if longing for the distant ocean. This, the previous owner told me on his brief tour of the house before fleeing north, was no problem. All I had to do was attach a garden hose to the tap at the bottom of the tank and drain out the water every six months. I could tell when it needed draining because I'd hear the well pump switch clicking on and off.

Of course, I put this off as long as possible, by which time the switch was playing the tarantella every time we took a shower. By now it was winter, and the hose, which I'd left out by the outdoor faucet, was frozen. I brought it indoors and it thawed out all over Zoë's carpet. Attaching it to the tank, I ran it through her bedroom (on the sub-ground floor, owing to the eccentric architecture of the house), through the garage, and down the garden. A chill wind knifed into the house through the open doors. The hose froze again before I could use it. I rolled it all up and waited for a thaw, and tried again. Success.

This worked for about six months, and then suddenly everything stopped: the well pump, which, thanks to its tarantella, had seen about one hundred and fifty years of wear and tear in less than a decade, burned out. We couldn't wash ourselves or our rapidly-growing heap of dirty clothes, couldn't use the toilet, couldn't make tea or coffee. . . . We became a household of itches in the scalp, stubble on the chin, and a scum of soft, pulverized food between the teeth.

The plumber came, and recommended a well guy; the well guy came and replaced the pump at slightly under a thousand dollars, but at least we had water again — except that it smelled of chlorine (as he had "shocked" the well to kill any bacteria), and it was black.

It looked as if someone had poured twenty gallons of ink into the well. The well guy didn't know what this murky black sediment was. The Health Department didn't know what it was, and confessed they wouldn't be able to test for anything useful anyway. We tried letting it stand for a day to see if the mystery contaminant would settle, which it didn't. Then we tried draining the well to see if the sediment would flush out.

I'd never drained a well before, needless to say. It sounded awfully apocalyptic to me, but all I had to do, apparently, was to run the hose from the bottom spigot on the holding tank out through Zoë's room again. . . .

Nobody had any idea how long it would take to drain the well; I'd just have to stand there and watch the hose.

That evening an unexpected visitor walking around the back of our house might have seen me relieving myself against a birch tree, next to a hose expelling a steady stream from the holding tank; and the visitor might have been struck, as I was, by these parallel acts of plumbing.

50

ESKER

We had lived in Essex Center for more than a year before we fought our way through the seven-foot-high reed canary grass to get to our woods, and then it took three attempts before we found our way through the woods and finally emerged through a fringe of young birches to find the heart of the valley.

It was breathtaking. Owing to a fluke of natural distribution, pockets of woodland hide not only the houses on Chapin Road, but also the houses on Old Stage Road, which runs parallel to Chapin Road up the other side of the valley. Standing among the milkweed, vetch, and knee-high grasses of this floodplain, the only other house you can see is several miles away, halfway up Bald Hill at the head of the valley. Only eleven miles from Burlington, but we could be in Maine.

Down the middle of the valley runs Alder Brook, named after the fringe of alders that accompanies it for almost its entire length. To the left, it widens out into a delightful pocket-sized swamp, mysterious and surrounded by evergreens, a perfect spot for moose. Nearby, a curious causeway or ridge, about eight feet high, parallels the brook. The top of the ridge is flattened, in part because the local snowmobile club uses it as a trail in winter, but what created this causeway originally? A long-abandoned cellar-hole full of blackberry bushes and some ancient and perplexing agricultural machinery made me wonder if this was the original road up the valley.

Nobody knew what it was. I certainly didn't connect it with an odd incident that had happened at the closing, when the attorney glanced over the deed to our new property and said casually that somebody seemed to have a right to gravel on our land. I'd never heard "gravel" as a verb — and in any case, what gravel? There's the driveway, of course, and I found a tiny pocket of gravel right where I wanted to put the vegetable garden, but barely a couple of cubic yards. In any case, the right had apparently not been exercised in thirty years, so we forgot about it.

None of this came together until I went to see Barbara Chapin, after whose family our road is named, and who has become the unofficial historian of the valley. She told me a great deal about her family and the other local families: the Bixbys, after whom the hill above us is named; the Cotas, who worked for her great-grand-father; and the Ferrands, another farming family who, when they first moved here one hundred and fifty years ago, bought a farm-house, sawed it vertically in half, hauled half of it to their land, lived in that half for a winter, then hauled the other half and shoved the two together around a huge tree stump that acted as a dining table.

The short road that runs across the valley, connecting Chapin Road with Old Stage Road, is called Colonel Page Road, after a Revolutionary-era spy turned double-agent who played both sides so successfully he ended up owning most of Essex. Barbara Chapin told me that her grandfather and the Ferrands used to gravel on both sides of Colonel Page Road, he on the Chapin land on the right by the Cota house, the Ferrands on the left. You can see it quite clearly if you know what you're looking for, she said, a gravel ridge that crosses the road—and immediately I knew what the "causeway" at the foot of our property was, and knew it was something I'd been fascinated by for thirty years. It was an esker.

When I was thirteen or fourteen, our geography teacher took a break from the tedious human geography of exports and imports and moved into the violent, dramatic stuff: geology. Volcanoes, earthquakes, clashing plates, extrusive vulcanicity, intrusive vulcanicity, the slow grind of glaciation ending in the crash of massive icebergs shearing off into the frigid waters of the poles. We copied diagrams of laccoliths and phacoliths, and we were shown photographs of the basalt hexagons of Giant's Causeway and, most mysteriously-named of all, drumlins and eskers.

I can still envision the drumlins (glacial in origin, method of formation uncertain) clearly, a dozen or more humps running across a field in Ireland, as if a school of whales were rising just beneath the sod. Eskers, too, were glacial, but a real freak of nature: they were the relic of an upside-down stream.

Ice melts under pressure, so many glaciers have a stream running under them—but instead of cutting down into the soil, like most streams, it wears away at the ice. As all streams carry sediment, this second-story glacial stream builds up a bed of silt and gravel above ground level, so when the glacier finally melts, the stream-bed is left behind as a meandering ridge, perfect for graveling and, in a later age, snowmobiling.

All my adult life I had wanted to see an esker, and now I owned part of one. I couldn't believe my luck.

A BIT GRAVELLY

If a driveway's job is to run from the garage to the road, the driveway doesn't exist any more. We simply can't get in and out of the garage; the turn's too sharp, the turning circle too small. From the day we moved in, our cars became the driveway's prisoners, exposed to sun, rain, snow and ice. I'm amazed that it took a year or more to face up to this, but as soon as I did so, the garage changed in two days into a tool-shed-cum-workroom-cum-game-room, and the foot of the driveway, the apron outside the garage, became an herb bed: basil, dill, and English lavender. The soil's a bit gravelly, but it gets the best sun anywhere on our land.

ALIEN GRAPE

Even before we moved out to Essex, I wanted a grapevine. Years
ago my mother had a vine in a greenhouse stuck on the back of a
house we briefly owned in England. The vine had been so important in some previous owner's eyes that the greenhouse had actually been built around the vine, a thick, barky growth that emerged
from the ground by the garden path and disappeared in through
a hole in the near wall of the greenhouse.

Once I started looking around, though, I realized I had all the
grape I needed, and then some. It grew up the Scotch pines in
the windbreak down the northern side of the house. It choked the
poor dying pear trees just down the hill, and it trailed down toward
my precious blueberry bushes. Above all, the first time I went for
a walk down our dirt road, pushing Maddy in her stroller, I was
stunned to see that it infested virtually every tree along the roadside, its useless grapes hanging down tantalizingly, its leaves being
chewed to shreds by Japanese beetles. I vowed that on the first cool
evening I would put on a pair of jeans and wade into the tree line
with my pruners and show the invader who was boss.

One Sunday, speckled with paint, I decided to end the day's work on a savage and vengeful note, and I set out loaded for grape. The first tree at the head of the driveway, I discovered, was not actually part of the tree line but a proud and solitary growth that had sprung up a good twelve feet from its neighbors. The grape had leaped across the divide not in single spies, as Shakespeare says, but in battalions, forming a continuous leafy cover eight feet off the ground. I clipped and hauled, and after a quarter of an hour the last clinging tendril lost its grip and joined a pile beside the road.

Until now I had been working at or above head height, but it was obvious that I needed to find out where the blasted grape was coming from. I tracked a slender, green vine back from its filament of leaves until it joined a brown artery as thick as my index finger. Now we were getting somewhere. This joined a thicker highway the diameter of my thumb, which I cut off with the pruner and dragged the severed end out of the branches above my head. Then I went back to the cut end, assuming that it would vanish into the ground. Instead, it joined a thicker vine, which in turn joined a yet thicker one, this grandfather as thick as my wrist and ancient with bark. I forced my way into the undergrowth and peered around. It went around this trunk here, then down here. . . .

Wait a moment. That wasn't a trunk. That was another grapevine. And that. And that.

57

I felt like Sigourney Weaver in *Aliens*, stumbling into the ghastly hatchery of monsters, looking for the alien and realizing that *it was all around her*. I had found the Mother Vine.

I must admit, there was an instant of horror. The grape twisted up on every side, and as I started to cut at this trunk and that, the freed vines jumped up at me and smacked at my head and hands. But I had started this in a fury and intended to keep that fury going, keeping half an eye on my pruners in case I accidentally severed one of the fingers of my left hand as I snapped and cut. Besides, I was new in the neighborhood, and I wanted to impress the neighbors as The Lone Forester, the only one on the road who had brought the grape to heel. I kept going, and the sour dust of grape bark filled my hair.

Extracting the vine by dragging it down out of the tree line was hard: a summer, perhaps half-a-dozen summers of growth and insinuation had left vines clinging to vines clinging to vines. Several times, the first thing to give was the original bough, dead and dry under the weight of its uninvited guest. On the other hand, if I cut the vine off at ground level and then hauled it out by the leafy end, there would be a moment of resistance and then the coiled, woody body would spring out at me like a serpent, forcing me to leap back into the road and putting me at the mercy of passing cars.

The calm summer evening became increasingly surreal, perhaps expressionistic, I don't know, the lowering sun stabbing through the trees, the road now littered with stray grape leaves, the grapevine gnarling out of the undergrowth or leering down from the trees with no sign of quitting. The roadside bank out of which the tree line grew started to seem more and more like the wasp's nest, and when I stepped on a fallen tree trunk it exploded under my weight, firing fragments of rotten wood and nameless burrowing insects all over my legs.

Finally, when I cut one stout, barky vine and threw my entire weight on it without any effect whatever, the true magnitude of the enterprise struck me. The blasted grape had reached the very summit of the tree, a good forty feet above the road. I let the sheared-off end fall from my hand, and it swung out over the road at windshield height. I couldn't even just leave the damn thing to die without running the risk of it decapitating someone. I reached up as far as I could and cut it, hoping that no basketball players on bicycles would cruise down our road during the next week or so.

By now I had about half a cord of grapevine piled up by the head of the driveway. I decided to leave the grape only half-defeated, as I had left the house half-painted. I went back inside to shower, and as the water hit my face and I shut my eyes, I imagined a fresh tendril of grape writhing up through the drain.

ALMOST
CONNECTICUT

Still trying to make up for cutting down the trees, I recently planted another replacement, not a knee-high baby spruce but a Norway Maple sapling, bought at a season's-end sale—a lovely thing, tall and slender, with purplish leaves. I dug the hole twice as deep as you'd think necessary, following the instructions in the pamphlet. I anchored it with grade stakes and wires made from coat hangers, and I watered it religiously. This tree not only would outgrow my guilt; it would also serve to block our view of our neighbor's house.

This is not just snobbery. Our neighbor's place is a classic Vermont dirt road sight: an unpainted simple wooden house, neither old nor beautiful but just cheap, squatting on a concrete foundation. You can tell it's unused, and was never intended for use, by the fact that it has no driveway. Instead, it's surrounded by weeds and by mechanical corpses: two trailers (one grandly calling itself the McCarthy Mobile Office), a rusted harrow and another unfamiliar piece of Jurassic agricultural machinery; a tiny, squat bull-dozer; a small maroon Dodge without windows, their frames duct-taped to patches of plastic sheeting; a white Cimarron, missing only one window but almost invisible in a thicket of goldenrod; a dozen or more tires; two small sheds, one incongruously sporting a dormer; half a dozen oil drums; a small, ancient, and very sorry snowmobile, its missing panels replaced with warped perf board, and another snowmobile in even worse condition, barely more than a snout with headlamps, and a motorbike in the same state as the snowmobiles; and a dozen piles of once-potentially-useful metal and wood oddments, a sort of builder's-supply savings account. The whole collection is undergoing a steady entropy, every year sinking farther into the soil, losing shape, purpose, and even meaning, making their way slowly back toward the periodic table of elements.

The sapling doesn't hide much of this, of course, and as soon as winter strips its leaves off, it won't hide any of it. In ten or fifteen years, though, it will have grown and filled out, and there'll be no sign of our neighbor's property. For all you'll be able to tell, we might live in Connecticut.

SICK HOUSE

This has been a sick house lately. First I had flu, which morphed into a sinus infection. Then Barbara had flu, which morphed into pneumonia, and a month later she's still coughing like a tubercular ghost and clutching at the lower lobe of her right lung, as if she's just been shot in a bad repertory play. Then Maddy had first a bad case of chickenpox and then an especially liquid case of a gastrointestinal infection that is galloping, so to speak, around northern Vermont. Exactly the time you don't want to lose all the water in your house. Again.

We have a new thousand-dollar well pump we're still paying for, but until recently we were stuck with the same old holding tank, up to its old on-and-off tricks. Finally, in a freelance writer's moment of relief and agony, I got a decent-sized check a month ago, and most of it went at once into paying off the new washing machine and having a new holding tank installed, a smart blue model—so smart, in fact, it had a cutoff switch that knew if the well was running dry and instantly turned itself off so that pump wouldn't burn out. I liked the sound of that.

Within days, the water was off again. Not a drop. The plumbers scratched their heads. Three possibilities, they said: 1. Leaky valve (cheap). 2. Failed well pump (another thousand dollars). 3. Well run dry. (I don't even want to think about that one.) They replaced the valve. Three days later, same again. They scratched farther down into the scalp, and replaced the cutoff switch. Two days later: no water again, and a child in gastric distress.

I've had it with wells. You can keep your hardy Vermont independence: give me town water and a sewer line.

The latest theory about the water is that it's actually an electrical grounding problem: the new washing machine, in a conspiracy of appliances, is somehow tripping the cutoff switch in the new tank. The entire house may need to be rewired. No wonder the previous owners moved to Alaska.

WINTER GEOMETRY

Some kind of large truck or pickup seems to have used our driveway to turn around. Huge, heavy tracks, a pair on each side, come halfway down then stop hard, leaving a crest, a stationary wake. It's amazing how deeply the tires have bitten into the surface.

It's very interesting, finding out what has been going on while you're not around—a little alarming, a little exciting. Over by the pear trees, a line of deer tracks crosses the bare soil where I recently put in daffodil bulbs. And in winter, once the back garden and the meadow are snowed over, we see deer, dog, squirrel, even mouse prints that give an entirely new sense of the valley, replacing the planner's patchwork of lots and boundaries. The first time I saw tracks that went straight across our back yard from one neighbor's property to the other's, everything changed. Parallel property lines, invisible fences, vanished. Winter had given us a new geometry.

When the snow melts, another track will appear in the brown and flattened grass. It'll run up the north side of the house, around the windbreak, and off toward our neighbors', the Viles. The dogs from up the road visit our compost heap so often during the winter, always following pretty much the same line, that they pack the snow down hard: the grass underneath is stunned, and takes longer to grow. For two weeks or more there's a parting of the blades, a fairy path. An animal driveway.

Aha! I've just realized that the marks on the driveway were the oil truck backing down far enough for his hose to reach our tank — and, as such, they're the first signs of winter.

MY LIFE IN
DRIVEWAYS

In John Cheever's story "The Swimmer," a young man decides to return to his home in Connecticut via all the swimming pools along the way. I find myself thinking of my life as a series of driveways, leading fitfully, in a series of shades of grey, to the present day . . .

1. *Heathview Road, Thornton Heath, London, England, 1953–1955*

I'm too young to remember. Vague recollection of a curve of terraced houses — row houses, they're called in the U.S. — built for pedestrians in the days of horses and streetcars and motor omnibuses and bicycles, an era before driveways when the front door was right at the kerb. We didn't have a car. Nobody in England did except my grandfather, who bought a Ford Consul, PUW 208.

2. *Stonard's Hill, Loughton, 1955–1960*

In an outlying London suburb, the classic British semi-detached house — that is, a brick duplex identical to a million others that were built between the wars when Britain's architects had clearly been to lobotomy school. It had a small (read: very small) front garden, a path to the front gate in the kind of broken-flagstone effect called "crazy paving," which my father laid while I stood around and watched a bee on a bush. The effect, then, was that an Englishman came out of his front door, passed through his tiny patch of rural-but-cultivated England, clicked open the symbolic gate, and was then in the public realm, the sidewalk, the public road, the pathway for the public vehicle — the bus, the trolley, the tram. The car hadn't yet forced these realms apart, nor started to turn the public road into a different definition of public, in which a torrent of private interests competed for space, and blamed the city for potholes.

Where were we supposed to put the car? On the road? In our case, the question was academic: my father had a motorbike — but where did he stable it? Wait, now I remember: several houses down, a path led round to the back of the houses on our road, between the (not quite as small) back yards and the plot of community gardens opposite, in England called allotments and in the U.S. called victory gardens. Some kind of prefabricated garage, made out of sheet asbestos and rusty L-girders, had been squashed into our back garden. He kept his motorbike there. That back alley was, in effect, our driveway.

3. Badgeworth Court, Badgeworth, 1960–1963

A minor stately home at the heart of a tiny village in the Cotswolds, converted into a group home for boys from broken homes, supervised by my parents. Here we had a driveway, a very significant one, both symbolic and functional. The driveway was for visits and deliveries, the coalman and other tradesmen going round to the tradesmen's entrances behind the kitchen, the visitors delivered by carriage up to the grand front door in its carved archway of sandstone, its tesselated marble flooring. This wasn't a house right out on the road to be stared at and even—horrors—dropped in on by any old passer-by. This was a late version of the Englishman's castle, his country seat.

Now I come to think of it, Badgeworth Court had an astonishing driveway. It was an extension of the little road that branched off the Shurdington-Churchdown road, ran down over Badgeworth Brook and then up to a small turning circle off which the whole of Badgeworth Village sprang: clockwise, Badgeworth Farm, Badgeworth Court, Badgeworth Church, and Badgeworth Manor. Our driveway, which was graveled in the traditional manner, began in the noble fashion that combined pomp with the echoes of war: with heavy gates and a gatehouse. In our day the handyman-gardener lived there; now the gatehouse has been re-done as if by Martha Stewart and is currently on sale for *a quarter of a million pounds*. The driveway curved between high hedges up to the front door, then headed uphill for thirty or forty yards, turned right beside one of the many ornamental yew bushes, ran parallel to the sunny south face of the house, with its many large sash windows and French doors, crossed the flight of stone steps that ran down the middle of the lawns, and ran round to the rear buildings—garage, stables, greenhouses. Anywhere that might need a delivery. Almost more a road system than a driveway—a feudal road system from the days when a house was almost a village in itself.

4. Athelstan Road, Worcester, 1963–1967

See #2. This city street was so unaccommodating for cars it wasn't even paved. It was actually a worse-than-dirt road, consisting of potholes and flints. A deterrent. Down the road and up into a vacant lot, some enterprising builder had put up a plaza of rent-out garages, and my father rented one—the one I hit with the wing mirror backing the car out when I was fourteen, still too young to drive legally. If we'd had a driveway and he could have parked on it, that wing mirror would still be alive today.

This was also an example of the Park And Walk tradition so common in England and so sacrilegious in the U.S., in which you have a garage or lock-up somewhere else—thus detaching the house from the car and defeating the very point of the driveway. The opposite of this is the London habit of paving over the tiny front garden so you can park your Mini on what was once your lawn. The rectangular driveway.

5. St. Andrew's Road, Malvern, 1967–1971

Our first driveway, running from a wooden double-pair of gates down to one of the prefab garages—lethal, brittle, prone to collapse—that were springing up all over England at the time. When I was a college student I got a summer job working in a concrete factory that turned out the sections from which these things were made. Ghastly job. Spraying latex on the raw concrete, then sprinkling different-color sand through a template so it looked from a great distance (Mars, say) that the garage was made of bricks.

Come to think of it, though, the fact that we had a driveway was a sign of the house's unusual history. We owned the end section of a large house once owned by the Earl of Blackmore, now divided vertically into three dwellings. There was no sign of a carriage

70

house, stables, or the relics of carriageways, but the property sur-
rounding the building had far more space than most houses in
which to lay out a driveway. And the middle section, of course, had
no driveway, so John Daniels next door had to park on the road or
Park and Walk. He parked and walked: I can still see him going out
through his front gate, turning right, and marching off toward the
station, his chin high, his bearing military. Strange to think that if
he had had a driveway, his very posture would have changed.

6. *Hallow Park, Hallow, 1971*

The crème de la crop of driveways, one that had been laid out for
no less a personage than Queen Elizabeth I. The original Hallow
Park had burned down late in the nineteenth century, but the
grounds were unaffected, and we could stroll down (or in my case,
be told to prune the hedges all along) the Elizabethan Walk. This
was a misnomer, because it was in fact the Elizabethan Ride, a carriageway that enabled Good Queen Bess, when she was staying at
Hallow for the hunting, to ride from the house along the ridge
overlooking the beautiful Severn Valley, down to the foot of the
grounds, around to the west, and up to the door of Hallow Church.
A double-hedge, thought to be almost unique, had been planted
along the view side of the carriageway in her honor, and I clipped
every inch of it.

7. Pembroke College, Oxford, 1971–1972

No driveways in central Oxford because it was still a city of pedestrians and (often very unskilled) cyclists. This car-free zone allows a wonderful transformation: you can be standing on the sidewalk in the hot sun, very much out in the world, people passing both ways, bikes propped up, cars out on the High Street, and then in a single step you can be in the cool, quiet, thoughtful embrace of the college. One single step.

8. Salisbury Crescent, Oxford, 1972–1974

See #2 again, though in this case the landlord's son, who lived in the converted attic, had parked an old Jaguar 2.4 liter, an Inspector Morse car, on the driveway, its engine lying in front of it so the carcass looked like a disemboweled deer. The whole front garden was essentially taken over by the car, and the needs of the road. Which is pretty much what a driveway does anyway, unless you have a *lot* of space.

9. Something Road, South Oxford, 1974

The end house in a row of terraced houses built for pedestrians in the days of horses and streetcars and motor omnibuses and bicycles. Just like Heathview Road, in other words, except that in the intervening twenty years everyone in England had bought a car. With no off-street parking or driveways, the road was lined on both sides by parked cars like an artery choked with plaque so, as with thousands of streets in England (and older neighborhoods in the U.S.), there was room for only one car at a time to squeeze through.

10. *Living/Learning Center, University of Vermont, United States of America, 1974*

A modern student dorm surrounded by an ocean of new asphalt. Even though the Center had been sited so students could walk from the dorm to main campus, this was the beginning of the era when almost every student would bring cars to campus. The tree-lined streets and the grassy quadrangles of New England college towns were doomed: from now on, all university buildings had their own driveways and parking lots. They also, therefore, had their own police and their own parking regulations. A parking ticket on the UVM campus can cost you as much as $150.

11. *310 Maple Street, Burlington, Vermont, 1974–1975*

A large Victorian house divided into at least half a dozen apartments, but with only one driveway running down the side. I

73

didn't have a car, but I imagine there must have been a lot of banging on doors and demanding that people move their frickin' vehicles. Nobody seemed to have told the landlord that if you subdivide a house you need a lot more parking space, though this was abundantly clear to the elderly lady who owned . . .

12. 200 *Maple Street, Burlington, 1975–1976*

A typical large old wooden family home converted into apartments, with front doors and staircases cut into every face and corner of the house. The stables had been converted to garages and the whole back (stable) yard had been paved over for parking, something that in 1900 would have seemed insane. Unimaginable.

13. *Converse Court, Burlington, 1976*

Can't remember. Didn't have a car. What I can remember is running outside with a gang of friends in the middle of a thunderstorm, throwing a Frisbee up and down the road in the torrential rain. How did we have room? Where were the cars?

14. *Grove Street, Oxford, England, 1976–1977*

The row house tradition once more, the front door and front window being one border of the sidewalk. In practice, this meant that a great deal of dust from the main road got in through my windows and settled on the ledges; but it also had that neighborhood quality of thinning the line between public and private, making me part of the neighborhood, whether I wanted to be or not. Interesting that this is now something we're afraid of: when we see a group of people hanging out talking on a street, they look like ne'er-do-wells, unemployed, thugs. The driveway has changed the street in this way, too, making it less of a public space.

By now I had a motorbike; I parked it in the pub car park next door. They didn't seem to mind.

15. *Tadley, Hampshire, 1977*

Not a clue. Can't remember the house. Can't remember why I was living there.

16. *Dean House, Dean, Hampshire, 1977–1978*

Another minor stately home. Baronial carriageway up to the grand front door. Cars parked in the cobbled stable yard round the back.

Fascinating experience to park your car in a stable that still looks like a stable: it feels as if the car is somehow snug, better cared for.

17. *Pamber Farm, Pamber, Hampshire, 1978–1979*

Eighteenth-century farm cottage. Parked my car on the concreted farmyard right outside the cottage's front door, parked my motorbike in a small outbuilding, whence it was constantly "borrowed" by the neighbor's kid without my knowledge. A long driveway ran past a duckpond, turned hard right, passed the front door of the next farm, then made a beeline for the road. The only place I lived in England where you had to go down to the mailbox at the end of the driveway to pick up your mail. I seem to remember the milk was left by the road, too, and the chickadees pulled off their famous trick of puncturing the foil tops with their beaks, then leaning down into the bottle and drinking the cream off the top.

18. *Shelley Close, Oxford, 1979–1980*

Another semi-detached #2, with a small but interesting difference: the driveway ran past the side of the house to the garage. This was a new development—there was no longer any pretense that the main thoroughfare took the visitor to the front door, like at

Badgeworth, in a triumphal arrival. This was now a house built in the Automobile Age, and there was no point in denying that the arriving homeowner was going to make for the garage, park, and then enter his castle by a front door that was no longer at the front but on the side, breasting the driveway. This new alignment made the garden seem more and more of an afterthought, like the plantings on traffic circles.

19. *Marston Close, Oxford, 1980*

The first place I lived that had been planned as a modern suburban—that is, car-driven—entity. This was the first place where I saw neighbors—almost all of them—washing their cars on a Sunday morning on the driveway out front, which turned the front yard into a showroom for the car. No gardens to speak of, just lawns. The English home in full retreat.

20. *Adsit Court, Burlington, Vermont, 1980–1981*

A typical American conversion: early-twentieth-century wooden house with driveway later added down side of building to garage, so we entered the house by the kitchen door. That, too, is an interesting development. I should go back and watch all those late

Fifties/early Sixties sitcoms, the Lucies and the Beavers, and see whether people came in through the front door or the kitchen door. As I recall, they still came in through the front door, at least on television: coming straight into the kitchen may have seemed too invasive and personal for the time, like climbing in through the bathroom window.

21. *South Winooski Avenue, Burlington, 1981–1982*

Another conversion, typical of the larger and older houses in town, in which the wooden carriage house out back had been turned over to car parking. You could easily tell from the road that this kind of conversion had taken place because the driveway was so steep. Virtually impossible to pull out onto the road without scraping your tailpipe.

22. *Silver Street, Monkton, Vermont, 1982*

A small, sagging rural house with some kind of wooden outbuilding intended as a nominal garage, though I always parked on the street or on the rutted dirt in front of the outbuilding. I had barely moved away before the "garage" collapsed.

23. *West Canal Street, Winooski, Vermont, 1982–1985*

Yet another early-twentieth-century wooden house, the driveway laid beside it back to the garage. This had a sad effect on the architecture of the house: because we always came and went by the side door, on the driveway, the front porch was never used, and served only to make the front rooms dark and gloomy.

Now that I come to think of it, a driveway is the opposite of a porch. The porch was designed as a halfway habitation: on the porch, the homeowner was sheltered and at home, but was also visible and available to passers-by, able to wave, call out, chat. The driveway assumes that you don't want to talk to passers-by, and that there aren't any anyway, as they're all in their cars. It means that instead of the intervening distance between private and public being small and joined by words, it is large, and one passes through it enclosed in a car.

24. *Barrett Street, South Burlington, 1985–1986*

This was the first raised ranch I lived in, and thus the first place where the car had essentially migrated indoors, like the pig in the Middle Ages, and you entered the house through the garage. A strange switch had thereby taken place: the triumphant or thankful homecoming, marked by a large, graceful doorway, was no longer the entry into the house. It was the entry into the garage, which could be made even more lordly and commanding by use of the remote door-opener. What this meant, in effect, was that the important moment was not when the master or mistress of the house came home. It was when the car came home.

25. *Catherine Street, Burlington, 1986–1987*

A neighborhood bungalow so small that the garage was larger than any of the rooms in the house. The driveway, even though it was only about twenty feet long, must have taken up almost 10 percent of the entire property.

26. *Gove Court, Burlington, 1987–1990*

Like #25, but very slightly larger. I'm trying to imagine what that pleasant leafy little corner of Burlington would look like in an era of bicycles and buses, the ugly garages pulled down, the driveways dug up. I see flower beds and small fruit trees.

27. *South Union Street, Burlington, 1990–1993*

Bizarre. Because it gets so much snow, Burlington insists on off-street parking, with all kinds of odd results, and this one takes the biscuit. I had to park in a tiny space under the front porch. If I didn't drive the nose of my car all the way into this earthy, stony, basementish hole, I got a ticket for having my rear wheels on the city sidewalk. But that was nothing compared to the issue of snow clearance. Every Vermonter expects to shovel snow, but I had nowhere to shovel it *to*. If I threw it to one side, it fell on our neighbor's driveway, and I got yelled at. I couldn't throw it out onto the road, as that was illegal, and in any case the plow would just pile it up across the entrance of my parking hole. If I threw it on the sidewalk, the same law applied, and it would be returned to me by the sidewalk plow. I had to stack it in thin columns as high as my head.

This house was also where I learned the dangers of on-street parking. One evening, around 5:45 p.m., I pulled up in front of the house, ran inside to get my teaching materials for my 6 p.m. class, and ran back out to find my car gone. Apparently the emergency brake had failed, and according to witnesses the car rolled calmly off on its own, pulled out into the busiest road in Vermont, picked a gap in the oncoming traffic, crossed the road, mounted the opposite curb, neatly picked its spot between a street sign and a tree,

81

rolled across a side street, pushed through a small hedge (large enough to slow it down, small enough to inflict no damage) and struck a wooden house at the exact midpoint between two studs so that the planking was stove in by a few inches, but neither house nor car was otherwise injured. This, my car was telling me, is why other people have driveways.

28. Marsett Road, Shelburne, Vermont, 1993–1994

Another tiny bungalow. The people who moved in after us brought with them one car, a huge pickup, and a boat, all of which are parked in the driveway. From certain angles you can't see the house at all.

29. Robinson Parkway, Burlington, 1994–1995

Garage built onto side of house, driveway from suburban street to garage, tiny footpath leading from driveway to front door with a little shrub next to it to boost its waning sense of grandeur and occasion. Mind you, the house illustrated another useful role of the blacktop driveway: as a basketball court. Unfortunately, not being a basketball fan, I wasn't thinking along these lines when I pulled up in the moving van and dinged the hoop several feet sideways.

30. *Chapin Road, Essex, Vermont, 1995–*

Home at last. The swimmer staggers, dripping, down the driveway, noticing for the first time that it too has its exact place in history. The house, built in 1973, is just one of the cheap suburban ranch houses that in the Seventies sprawled out into the sticks where the land was cheap, the first wave of the erosion of rural Vermont. And as such it has the short simple driveway of the suburbs, road to house, just like that. The builder didn't even give any thought to its steepness, and the problems that would inflict on a succession of owners. Driveways were just driveways. Ten years later, as house and land prices boomed, only the rich could afford to move out toward Nature, and they demanded palatial houses with bay windows and cathedral ceilings and long baronial driveways winding fifty, a hundred yards from the road as if their house were Badgeworth Court or Hallow Park, and any day now Good Queen Bess would visit.

The swimmer sees all over again how difficult and out of place this token, ridiculous little driveway is, how weedy, how not-gray. With all his other houses and driveways fresh in his mind he has the odd feeling that his present driveway is sinking out of sight beneath the country soil, that in a few years' time it may be little more than two parallel impressions on the resilient grass.

YEAR THREE

POLLEN

Taking a break from mowing in order to clear up some of the debris on what I claim will be a lawn, I hurled a dead branch into the Scotch pines that constitute the windbreak on the north side of the house, and where it hit the nearest tree, a cloud of yellow dust fell from the cones and drifted slowly away. I was fascinated and yet appalled. At this time of year, if it's not pollen, it's seed: any area of the flower beds that I weed down to bare earth starts sprouting one rapacious weed or another almost at once, overtaking and choking my own little seedlings. These days, on a calm, clear evening the view across the valley is hazy with innumerable specks, and columns of insects rising and falling as they drift north across the thickets of reed canary grass, vetch, and goldenrod.

On humid days, the air seems so thick I can almost chew it. It feels as if my lungs will have to sieve through this invisible yet almost tangible bioactive cloud, like a small boat shoving through waterweed, to get to each oxygen molecule. Zoë, now eleven, is already needing antihistamines every so often; I dread the thought of Maddy, now three, inheriting my asthma.

Spring in our valley, this airborne season, is life at its most irrepressible; but it's also the one thing that I can imagine driving us out of here.

CAR MESS

It's a little late for spring cleaning, but who am I to argue? At long last Barbara has cleaned out her smelly, mistreated Toyota, a process that took two days and violated several hazardous waste ordinances. The shoe is now on the other foot; I'm the one who is the butt of the messy-car sarcasm, and I don't like it at all.

Still, the unexamined car is not worth driving, so let's consider what we're actually talking about here. Let's see what evidence the car offers of the way I live, the impact I have on my unfortunate surroundings. I pull the Volvo down to the foot of the driveway and compile an inventory. In the front of the car:

—an empty, half-crushed carton of chocolate milk;
—an empty juice bottle, the label mysteriously missing;
—a pair of blue plastic pliers from a child's carpentry set, the jaws stuck together with a livid purple mass, the remains of a small unlikely monster that Zoë made in clay for Maddy and didn't have time to bake before Maddy took it to play with in her car seat; it got left

on the dashboard in the full sun and melted into the
heater vent;
—two leaflets: "New Tree Planting" and "Insects and
Diseases";
—a receipt for one Sensation Lilac ($34.95) and one Pur-
ple Leaf Sand Cherry, two gallons ($23.95);
—a pencil with the head of a troll;
—two bent drinking straws;
—thirty cents in change: the rest Maddy mailed into my tape
deck, which now, to nobody's surprise, does not work;
—a stick from a Dove bar and another from a lollipop;
—a receipt from the dump, attached to which is a strange
hard lump of some whitish substance, possibly the
butt-end of a very old stick of mozzarella cheese;
—two more receipts from the dump;
—a Dunkin' Donuts paper napkin;
—a nearly-empty bottle of spring water;
—an empty packet of alphabet pretzels;
—a giant blue Lego-on-wheels;
—countless animal cracker limbs and torsos;
—a Tom Waits tape, "The Heart of Saturday Night,"
minus its box;
—a Richard Thompson tape, "Small Town Romance," ditto;
—Zoë's book report on book seven of the Animorphs series

("Cassie is important to this book because she likes to
make sure that everything seems right and she double
checks everything. This saves them time and again from
the yeerks");
—a music box in the shape of a blue-and-yellow plastic television, no maker's name, the bar code label saying only
"Pre-School Toy/L $4";
—another blue-and-yellow plastic music box, this time
a Sesame Street product that plays "People in Your
Neighborhood";
—two dozen or more family photographs: the one on top is
of our friends Bert—that is, Bertha—and Jeff leaning
on the rail of the deck behind our house next to Barbara, who is holding Maddy in the crook of her left arm,
while with her right she appears to be making the American Sign Language sign for "the flying boat is about to
touch down";
—the plastic wrapper from a stick of mozzarella—aha!
a smoking gun!
—a light blue sock of Maddy's;
—a children's book called *Who's Wearing My Sunglasses?*
whose pages you turn, rather disturbingly, by poking
various animals in the eye;
—an empty cider bottle;

91

—wraparound kid's sunglasses;
—bark mulch;
—paper clips;
—pine needles; and
—gravel.

That's just the front of the car. The back is a *real* mess.

SQUIRREL IN
THE MAIL

Walked up to fetch the mail, and discovered that overnight a spider had taken over the mailbox, converting it into a giant trap. I wondered what the carriers do under such circumstances, and went down to the post office to ask.

The chap on the counter didn't know—I hadn't realized what a deep distinction exists between carriers and counter clerks—but he said, "Want to hear a strange story about a mailbox? How about a dead squirrel in one?" A homeowner called the post office to say that some unknown felon had run over a squirrel, killing it, and had stuffed the corpse in the nearest mailbox. His, that is.

It was an odd moment, because I couldn't tell what kind of emotional flag he was hanging on the end of his story. I half expected him to use the kind of indignant tone that implies, *That mailbox is government property. We can't allow people to go around stuffing dead squirrels in our mailboxes, now can we?* Or possibly a friends-of-animals tone that implied, *What a heartless bastard this must have been, adding insult to injury.* But he seemed almost gleeful, in a suppressed way, as if the actual mailboxes were the wild frontier of his office's otherwise mundane activities, the line of interface between civilization and chaos, and this was another in an occasional series of enlivening yarns about the bizarre things that happen out on the dirt roads, the rural routes.

LAUREL AND HARDY

It's a classic trap, like the bucket of water falling on the head as you open the door. It's Laurel and Hardy.

"Would you like a piano?" Barbara's friend Bert—Bertha, that is—asked her. Bert knew someone in Fairfax who had one, never used it, the old story. Sort of a permanent loan, a good home to go to, two children and a musical household, you need one. Bring civilization to Essex Center. Only cost you the shipping. Sure, Barbara said. Sounds great.

I growled and humphed. Maybe. What sort of shape is it in? Spotting the shape of the bucket already on the top of the door, knowing the cost of moving a piano from Fairfax to Essex.

Bert says it's fine, she said. Bert is a music teacher. Knows a decent piano if she sees one. Impeccable reference.

Well, maybe, I say, still thinking we should probably look at it first.

Next thing I know, Barbara has booked the movers, the instrument is due to arrive at noon. No sign. 2 p.m. No sign. Two-thirty, three. The truck arrives, and backs cautiously down the driveway.

They can't get a direct run from the back of the truck to the front porch. We move railroad ties, sculptural boulders, wheelbarrow, garbage, hose, the ten thousand other summer accoutrements that I still haven't got around to putting away. The truck finally edges around into position. The piano is heaved out. My mouth falls open. The bucket of water lands on my head.

I wasn't expecting a Steinway. Nor a Baldwin. Nor even a top-of-the-line Yamaha. I wasn't expecting a grand, or even a baby grand. On the other hand, I was not expecting birdshit.

"Yeah, this was in the barn," say the movers. "Looked as if it had been there for years." Later I discover that Bert hadn't actually *seen* the piano . . .

Dark shapes and forces move in my brain, which has become overloaded with thick, treacly, deep emotion and is working with unaccustomed slowness, so I fail to grasp this chance to slip them a quick fifty and ask them to haul it back into the truck and accidentally misdeliver the piano to the landfill. I am still trying to imagine what ghastly wreckage will have befallen the godforsaken instrument after a decade or two between the hay bales and the rodents.

I stagger back indoors. The movers, meanwhile, are working with equally treacly slowness to try and figure out how to get the piano inside. The front deck is small, the mudroom-cum-hall is small, the stairs start at once, the turn is tight. . . . One of them unpacks his Cray, runs a few calculations on PianoMove 2000, and determines that the piano (a) cannot be moved by the three movers we have engaged and (b) will not make the turn from the front hall up the stairs to the living room. The program also calculates that instead of costing us $150 the move will cost us more than twice as much, and it begins radio-carbon-dating the decaying finish on the instrument's woodwork before the mover switches it off.

Time passes. More strange dark shapes and patterns shift deep in my brain. The fourth mover arrives, and at last a lobe of my brain detaches itself from the task of plotting revenge and realizes that if we dismantle the fake wrought-iron railing from round the woodstove the piano can be rolled in on a ramp so easily that we won't even need the fourth guy, who is now on the payroll and engaged in the familiar yes-it-will-no-it-won't-maybe-if-we-stand-it-on-end debate with his colleagues. We dismantle. We ramp. The piano is wheeled into place and, missing its back legs or casters, is leaned gently against the wall, like a dying wildebeest.

The Cray spits out a bill the size of the GNP of many small nations, it occurs to me that it will cost just as much to get rid of this vast musical carcass, and the movers leave. A silence descends, like the one after the eruption of Vesuvius. I tap a key, experimentally: it makes a faint thudding noise and stays down.

Okay. Chin up. I rally the troops. The first operation on the piano will not be to play "Heart and Soul" after all, but to scrub off the mud and the guano. We assemble buckets, scrubbers, Earth Friendly Gentle Guano Remover, etc., and set to work on the woodwork, which has that leathery, crocodilian finish of old varnish that has seen a new century and doesn't like it. At one point Zoë opens the lid and we discover a spider the size of a Pekinese. And that, more or less, is the story so far. This week, a piano restorer (recommended by the regular tuner-guy, who took one look at the innards and backed away, making the sign of the cross with his fingers) will come and look at it and answer a simple question: will this thing cost more to repair than to remove? In odd moments, I examine the joints carefully to work out if I could hack it apart with a hatchet, strap the frame to the roof rack, and drive it to the dump.

The cheap upright piano is said to have civilized America; in many pioneer Plains households, it was not only the sole musical instrument, it was the only piece of finished furniture. The girls bang away at ours, and it makes the discordant, booming sound of a steel mill undergoing its annual industrial cleaning. We have not brought civilization to Essex Center.

LUMPY ARMCHAIR

When I was a boy I had a recurring dream that gravity had failed, and I was floating helplessly upwards into the unfathomable lonely blue of the sky. I spent the first half of my life moving, over and over again, almost compulsively. Now I'm imagining digging a pond in the meadow and building a pair of gateposts athwart the driveway like the entrance to a Japanese temple, and in the meantime I'm planting fruit trees and bushes—literally putting down roots. Being in a foreign country has made my gravity seem all the weaker, and I suspect that wanting to learn about the history and botany of this valley, even to the absurd point of studying my driveway, is probably an attempt to draw sustenance from this foreign soil, to wriggle and settle into its ecology as if it were a lumpy armchair. Hoping that by learning and adapting to its contours I can finally relax into the afternoon of my life.

WALNUT BRAIN

Grrrragh! I've just discovered another reason to hate winter: cat shit. There's still six to eighteen inches of snow everywhere on our land, with the sole exception of the couple of square yards above the septic tank and the tire tracks down the driveway, where the gravel is soft and oozing during the day, but solid at night. Very scenic and all, but it means the cats can't shit outside, which means they have to use the litter box in the laundry room outside my office, which means we have to remember to empty it twice a week, which we don't, so just now I caught Ernie, the dumb one, shitting in a corner in my office—and then, as if to add insult to insult, scratching up some of my papers in a primitive, walnut-brained attempt to hide the evidence. I yelled at him like I haven't yelled at a sentient being for years, chased him out, scooped up the shit, cleaned out the cat box, refilled it, threw the plastic bag onto the diminishing snow bank on the deck, tossed some handfuls of seed down for the birds. Now I'm back in my office, trying to work with the window open to dispel the smell, furious. Simmering and freezing.

SNOWS

Just as I was about to get into the car I noticed that it was snowing one of my favorite snows, the brilliant little individual snow crystals falling out of a clear blue sky when the temperature drops below minus ten, like tiny petals manifested by Indian swamis; and it struck me that not only are no two snowflakes alike, but no two snowfalls are alike.

Legend has it that the Inuit have names for every kind of snow, and I found myself wondering if this were really true. So I dipped into a few pages of James Halfpenny and Roy Ozanne's *Winter: An Ecological Handbook*, and at once found myself among experts. Any culture that has a word *(qali)* for "falling snow that gathers on tree branches" knows what a magical transformation occurs for the exquisite hour or two after the snow has stopped and the dark evergreens are brilliantly etched in white.

There's poetry here, too. The Russian term *sastrugl*, meaning a sharply-etched and wind-eroded snow surface, conveys the hiss of frozen ice granules blowing over the crust, followed by a slight shiver. The Inuit term for "falling snow" is *annui*, which at least conveys the sense of tedium of long winter afternoons, and I also like the Inuit for drifting snow, *siqoq*, which apparently means "smoky."

Some of the Inuit and Dindye words are masterpieces of compression: a phrase such as "space formed between drift and obstruction causing it" boils (so to speak) down to *anmana*, "irregular surface caused by differential erosion of hard and soft layers" can be summed up as *tumarinyiq*, and "bowl-shaped depression in snow around the base of trees" is more neatly said as *qamaniq* in Inuit and *zhe-guin-zee* in Dindye. "Snow deep enough to need snowshoes" is *det-thlok* in Inuit, though there's no term for "snow deep enough to need snow tires" or "snow deep enough to cancel school."

In fact, after just a couple of pages of Halfpenny and Ozanne I couldn't stop thinking of all the words we don't have for the snows we do:

— the braided, twisting strands of snow granules that blow across the interstate in the slipstream of tractor-trailers;
— Zamboni snow, actually ice shavings, piled outside the hockey rinks even in midsummer;
— driver's seat snow, the small, annoying flurry sucked into the interior of the car when you open the door first thing in the morning;

—snow ghosts blowing off roofs on brilliant cloudless
mornings;
—charcoal crusts of ploughed urban snow at the end
of three straight weeks of sub-zero weather;
—melting urban snow reeking of thawing dogshit;
—the first snow of winter, a light, surprising snow that
drifted sporadically out of a sky that had only moments
earlier looked like rain, falling tentatively here and
there, melting at once, harmless, nostalgic, reminding
people of the possibilities of a little cross-country skiing
or of screaming down the hill at the foot of Underhill
State Park on an inflatable snowtube;
—cold, wet, nasty, clinging snows that are the bad-tempered
cousins of rain, leaving you with perpetually wet feet
from trudging through slushy puddles in sneakers;
—flat-out, whiteout blizzards scouring across the fields and
roads, closing the interstate, making country roads vanish
whenever they pass an open windward field, leaving driv-
ers cursing, wiping, steering by dead reckoning, guessing
the midpoint between the silhouettes of two sets of trees;
—the biting microscopic hail that sands away at the cheeks
and makes me glad to wear glasses;
—the blowing upward snow, like confectioner's sugar,
that swirls in tiny devils;

103

—the mean-spirited, stingy little flakes of ice that the wind spits across the fields, almost more of a wind than a snow, a wind chilling at twenty below zero, an old, old wind remembering its days of unchallenged ascendancy over the woolly mammoth and the cave man, a wind of endless glaciers and frozen black mountains, a wind that knows itself to be not a weather but an element.

YEAR FOUR

SPRING TAX

I wonder if April 15 was selected as tax day specifically so as to arrive with spring.

A fiscal year is a moveable feast, so they could have made it January 1, or June 1, but instead they chose it so it coincided (up here, at least) with the daffodils. Perhaps someone thought that, if your tax calculations left you with a rebate, it would seem a timely reward, a bulb planted last year, arriving with the sun. And if the news were bad, this would seem like a time of renewal, when life and hope spring eternal, and no bad news could possibly last.

Which perhaps explains why, after learning that I owed the I.R.S.—are you sitting down?—some *eleven thousand dollars*, I found myself spending the first warm weekend of the year out in the garden.

Part of me wanted to cancel spring. *Owing to unforeseen financial circumstances, there will be no spring this year. Summer and fall will be collapsed into three weeks, and winter will begin seven months early.* I couldn't afford to buy any shrubs or fruit bushes. No topsoil, no potting soil, no compost, no peat moss. No seedlings, bedding annuals, or landscaping timbers. No replacement for the dead pear tree, withered in infancy.

Instead, I tottered around outdoors, trying to clear my head. The daffodils were coming up everywhere, the grape hyacinths, the tulips. It was not only a time of discovery, it was a time of discovering good things that happened in their own good time, with little or no help from me. Bulbs in particular have the perfect ability to rewrite history in a positive light: the ones that come up are a shout of joy and a reward for foresight and hard work; the ones that don't come up—I've always forgotten that I planted them anyway.

Late last summer I broke open dozens of dried lupin pods and scattered the small black seeds on a patch of scrubby earth I wanted to rehabilitate. Nothing happened. Watered them. Weeded. Nothing. Gave them up as a bad job. This weekend, dragging my sorry soul past the scrubby patch now rapidly being taken over by grass, clover, milkweed, and other outlaws whose names I never intend to learn, I spotted the tiniest coronet of lupin leaves barely above ground, each ray of leaves holding a single drop of rain like a small child holding a large transparent marble. Then another, then half a dozen more. A couple of hours' weeding and some patience, and I'll have my lupin bed after all, costing nothing.

That was the theme for the weekend: something from nothing.

Barbara and I dug up some very old two-by-eights from the wood-pile beside the driveway, relics of a bunk bed I made for Zoë seven years ago, and made Maddy a sandbox. Forking over last summer's herb bed I discovered that lavender and rosemary had survived, so I potted them up and set them up on the deck. And in the garage, a couple of dozen packets of seeds, a tax-free inventory I had forgotten.

Around the back of the house, the concrete foundation was already half-hidden by a spray of light green—yes, that's right: last fall I broke up the thicket of daylilies and dotted the rhizomes here and there with little expectation that the little dusty nut-like swellings would ever really sprout, but they had done me proud. If the taxman was saying I had less than I needed, the garden was telling me I had more than I knew what to do with.

Even the indoor plants were determined to pay dividends. The two grapefruit trees that I have grown from seeds, which over the winter had gone into a kind of latitude shock and had had most of their lowest leaves nibbled off by our house rabbit, turned out to be throwing new clusters of leaves from what seemed to be dead wood. I took them outside and immediately, obligingly, it rained a warm spring rain.

SEVENTEEN WAYS OF LOOKING AT A DIRT ROAD

1. Nobody every moved to Vermont because of its well-paved roads. We still have a higher percentage of unpaved roads than almost any other state. Dirt roads are a light footprint on the land, the most minimal concession to the automobile, the ragged fringe between civilization and wilderness. "The crooked unimproved roads," wrote Blake, "are the roads of genius." I love them. This is my gravel cadenza, my ode to inconvenience.

2. A dirt road has history on its side. Most of the world's roads are dirt. Even in the United States, nearly two-thirds of the rural mileage consists of dirt roads; in Vermont fewer than half of all roads, rural and urban, are paved. The dirt road was here first, and it will endure. It is the once and future road.

3. Dirt roads are a communal creation, not suffering from the autocracy of engineers. "A lot of 'em were never designed in the first place," said Bob Niles, dirt road expert for the state of Vermont. "They evolved. From a cow path to an ox-cart path to a horse track to a buggy road to an automobile road. And back then there wasn't the means to move material, so they used what was close by, not what was good. They put stone fences and trees in the middle, and in a lot of places they're still there, and you've got a road built on decaying trees, or you've got stones working up through to the surface." In the late Fifties, Chapin Road had a huge chunk of ledge sticking up in the middle of the road, up at the Westford end. Too big to move, not worth blasting, so they just left it there. The grader went around it. The school bus went around it. Chapin Road was the perfect hybrid: half road, half part of the landscape. A dirt road is a long-running experiment in sustainable transportation.

4. A dirt road can have its own dimensions. As soon as you pave a road, you widen it at least to the breadth of the paver. A dirt road can be as narrow as it likes—and the dirt road that is also the main road from Brookline, Vermont, to neighboring Athens, for example, likes to be pretty narrow, climbing through woodland, narrowing as the valley and the brook beside it narrow, until finally it

111

squeezes between a pair of large rocks. Try that with a paver and you'd have to rip out half the landscape —which is, of course, exactly what has happened, most places.

5. A dirt road knows its place, and doesn't claim to own all it sees. It's still obedient to the rise and fall of the land, to the extrusions of rock and the subversions of water. It nudges small ponds and stream, and it brushes under low branches; it holds together a fine old sugarhouse, upland meadows, some neat modern architecture, a few tottering shacks —there's nothing like a dirt road to demonstrate, without condescension, the diversity of the state, to assert its democracy.

6. A dirt road doesn't suggest the same sense of urgency as a paved road, the same frowning narrowness of purpose. A dirt road asks to be walked on, like a lane —and as soon as you start walking, you start noticing things, like the small bunches of hard green elderberries, the irises in the ditch. And as soon as you notice those things, you are part of the countryside, and the cars that pass seem hasty and hard. You are outside the box.

7. A dirt road is interactive: it acknowledges our progress in a cloud of dust, or in the curling lip of a rut. With a dirt road, we are someone: we do not pass unnoticed or unremembered. Consequently,

a dirt road is a panorama of clues. I can tell if the mail has come by examining the shoulder next to the mailbox: if the mail carrier has already been through, there's a tire track that emerges from the general well-pressed surface of the road's core, curves over to the box, and where she pauses, the weight of her SUV leaves a discernible ripple, a good inch deep, two or three inches in April. The tread-ridges from her tires are sharp and fresh; the mail is here. And the road gives as good as it gets. My Volvo has rust spots blooming on the doors and wheel arches like canker sores, drawn out by age, mud, and road salt. This seems fair: the car takes its toll on the road, and the road takes its toll on the car.

8. A dirt road is a reminder that the intersection between the human world and the natural one is lethal. At the head of the driveway, on the way back from visiting the chickens at Chapin Orchard, Maddy and I find a garter snake, white belly up, flattened into a treble clef. I've seen at least dozen dead garter snakes on Chapin Road, not to mention worms, mice, butterflies, peepers, chipmunks, rabbits, cats, groundhogs, birds beyond identification, and insects beyond number. They are the true cost of driving. On tarmac they look out of place, as if the animal were simply stupid, or a trespasser, and in any case the remains are soon erased. On my road they are unmistakably my neighbors, whom I need to watch out for. Their skin and juices become part of the road.

9. Dirt roads are self-policing: you can't go all that fast on a surface that creates its own speed bumps. The joyriders who career past our house in the middle of the night may sound as if they're flying, but I'd be very surprised if they're going more than fifty. It's hard to stay on the road at that speed, and even harder to keep your car from falling apart. A dirt road, then, enforces humility.

10. A dirt road is different every day. Winter makes every corner and hill an event, each producing a small tightening of the stomach. In early spring, underground frost cells begin to thaw, areas of road the size of soup plates turn to sandy porridge. Just across the line into Westford, entire roads, even schools, are closed for mud. Walking down the road on a warm Easter day I've heard the road hissing as streams of tiny bubbles rise and break in the thin film of water on the crown of the road. One morning I stood on our road talking to Bridget Meyer, watching her feet: every time she shifted her weight, a patch of road four feet away from her sighed. In summer the road hardens and dries to the color of putty, but even then a single downpour changes its topography, leaving it open and available to surprises. One morning I saw a flash that was three goldfinches rising, startled, from a pothole, as if I had stumbled across the end of an invisible feathered rainbow. By early October, the first few leaves have fallen into the ruts and ditches that in two weeks will be full of crisp fragments slowly losing their vivid color, softening and turning to mulch.

11. Dirt roads don't lie. A paved road—a "good" road—underlies us like a safe assumption, its smooth silence reassuring us that this is where we and our car belong. But a car doesn't belong anywhere. It's only a native species in the fictional world in which we are masters of the earth. A dirt road doesn't respect this fiction. If we want to believe in our ascendance over our surroundings the last thing we want is a rude series of jolts that remind us otherwise. A dirt road doesn't lie obedient and supine; it calls attention to itself. Here in wet weather the rain runs out of the fields down the sides of the roads in streams a foot or two wide, then washes sideways down the riverbank and into the brook, carrying road with it. Nothing is flat or level: the crown of the road is hard washboard or one long trough of liquid brown sand, sucking and clutching at the tires, the steering wheel twitching in my hands. There's a gravel road in Ryegate so steep that in winter they have to sand it from the top, the sanding truck edging down backwards, so the truck drives on the sand it has just scattered. Otherwise it'd just bog down or slide right into the ditch. The town—and this would be heresy anywhere else—has gasoline trucks instead of diesel because a diesel engine is so much heavier that as the truck backs downhill the front end would slide right round. A mechanical pirouette, a ballet for dirt roads in winter.

12. A dirt road is a philosopher's avenue, a garden of time and change. Building a road—in Vermont, at least—is all about water.

115

Road engineers talk about wanting to prevent "the migration of the fines," the tiniest particles of soil. Whenever it rains, the fines migrate, not only downward but sideways or even up, especially in spring. Paving a road is the perfect emblem of the human endeavor to stamp something solid and permanent on the face of continual change. The dance along the artery, the circulation of the lymph — these are the migration of the fines. The trickle of water in the ditch, carrying its freight of protozoa, algae, tiny fragments of silica, quartz, gneiss, schist, granite — this is the migration of the fines. The cell-by-cell advance of the pine root, the chipmunk scurrying across the dead leaves — these are the fines in migration. When we talk about roads, what we think of proudly as "building" is actually the opposite of creation: in the name of business and efficient locomotion we prevent growth and change, we arrest the migration of the fines. Paving a road, then, is a kind of vanity: we believe we can prevent change — but as change is life, road-paving also involves a kind of death. Or our best attempt at it, because the pavement will eventually crack, the valve leak, the car rust.

13. A dirt road is part of everything else. Today, small potholes full of muddy water run in lines down the road like the ripples of skipped stones. A red sports car hits a pothole with a *smack!*, spraying water and road everywhere, and now that I look more closely each pothole in this chain has a sandy smear feathering away to

the right where the road surface has literally gone west. The rain has converted a tire rut into a tiny brook, whose gravel bed, no more than three inches wide, wriggles down toward the edge of the road—and thence to Alder Brook, to Indian Creek, to the Winooski, to Lake Champlain, to the Richelieu, the St. Lawrence, and the world.

14. Each dirt road has its own sound: the satisfying crunch of tiny particles of gravel underfoot, the scuff of dust.

15. Mending a dirt road is a rural art. You can't patch potholes in a dirt road, you have to scrape down below them with a grader, push the entire surface aside and then spread it all back again, leaving it red and raw as rope burn. In mud season the public works office puts up the signs saying NOTICE NO VEHICLE HAVING A WEIGHT and sends out the grader according to the weather forecast: if he's a day too early and the temperature is rising, the heavy equipment of the road crew will do more damage than they mend; if he's a day too late the temperature may have fallen by fifty degrees, the washboard ridges are hard as concrete, and we'll be stuck with them for another six weeks.

16. Once paved, a dirt road loses any sense of local identity: it is now like any other new paved road, its color a tint not found in nature. Paving is not a construction but a theft, as if a line had been

117

drawn by a giant eraser rubbing out color, texture, past, and future, leaving only a kind of solid shadow over which our wheels pass noiselessly as we speed to work. It also steals the road's history, for the job of a paved road is not to be noticed, and something we don't notice has no history.

17. A dirt road is a living thing, echoing and responding to the land rather than flattening it, reflecting in its color the soils of people's farms and back yards. A dirt road is not the triumph of civilization over nature, but a calm contentment, a cohabitation.

IN GOOD TIME

I came home at lunchtime after a typically frantic morning getting to classes on time, meeting students on time, checking email, checking voicemail, calling home to check the answering machine, trying to make things happen as quickly as possible in order to buy myself some time, somewhere down the road.

As soon as I got home I had to put two coats of polyurethane on all the pieces of wood that would make up Maddy's assemble-it-yourself swing set, which I had to get done that afternoon, as the good weather was due to break. I moved with controlled haste, laying out all the slats and uprights on the driveway so I could stain them all with the least turning-over and the fewest movements of the can ... but was brought up short by the fact that nothing I could do would make the first coat dry any more quickly than it wanted to. It would dry in its own good time.

What is good time, though? I wondered, sitting on a patch of weeds that had forced its way up through the gravel. Good time is the recognition that there are valuable processes whose rates are beyond our control. I can't do anything about the surface tension of the brush or the viscosity of the stain, both of which affect how much stain the brush will hold, just as I can't affect how rapidly the wood absorbs stain, or how rapidly the sun and wind dry it. Good time takes into account the subtlest and tiniest of entities—cells, atoms—respecting them all for their rates of activity, indifferent to none. God's time, in a way.

Nowhere do I lose sight of good time more importantly than in myself. I may know from experience how long a painted pine two-by-four takes to dry, but how much work can I expect from myself in a day? How many phone calls can I answer? How many other people's well-being can I worry about? My body, consisting of natural processes, has its own good time, too. I can take in data up to only such-and-such a bit-rate, then I have to start shutting down systems to cope: the humor system, the intimacy-and-emotional-openness system, the alertness-to-others'-feelings system, the awareness-of-my-own-breathing system, the digestive system, the immune system.

So this is what I thought as I sat on the driveway, gradually becoming aware of the warm breeze and the scudding clouds. And pretty soon the first coat was dry.

SPLIT RAIL

Since spring, the split-rail fencing around the landing at the head of the driveway has fallen apart. The steady shifting of subsoil and rain has left the posts leaning farther and farther out of the vertical until one by one the rails disengage from their slots and fall with a woody thump. This fencing is among the most beautiful things on this property. Covered with gracefully-frilled blots of lichen, yellow, white, light green, a delicate ash-gray, and small rugs of emerald-green moss. Even the wood itself has taken on colors: underneath, the rails are the weathered gray of a barn about to fall in on itself; on top they are all shades of watery grey-green.

Part of me wants to restore this fencing, which runs around two sides of the landing, to re-dig the post holes, maybe even set them in a little concrete, slot the whole thing back together, tap in an inconspicuous little nail or two here and there to help. After all, this is irreplaceable. Lichen is the slowest-growing living organism; these rails have earned their mottled decoration.

Yet this is really a core human vanity, to want to arrest time and change while at the same time enjoy its effects, like wanting to be

121

wise but still young, like wanting a 1953 MG that actually runs. There's a kind of noble authenticity about the fallen timbers, like the abandoned stone fence down at the foot of the meadow, now almost invisible behind the scrub of small trees that has grown up around it.

This fence, like anything artificial, blooms twice: once when it's brand new, and once when it finally gives up the struggle to be useful, and gives in to forces that are stronger and more patient.

SNOWBLOWER
ORNAMENT

After the first real snowfall, sixteen inches in twenty-four hours, I met Tom Blanchard, our neighbor from across the road. He had just arrived at the foot of his own driveway (which is so long we've never actually seen his house, just his driveway winding away out of sight up over the ridge), riding a lawn tractor with a snowblower attached. He's a big man, and he was wearing heavy overalls, a hat, and earmuffs, and on that little conveyance he looked like a gorilla sitting on a roller skate. He immediately offered to plough our landing, and then he overrode my protests and ploughed a four-foot-wide path down the driveway to the house, which would become invaluable over the next four days as a further foot of snow fell. I've barely said a word to him in three and a half years; we meet only at times of need, and he helps me out, waves cheerfully, and disappears for another nine months.

How do you thank someone who ploughs your driveway but doesn't want to be paid? Right before Christmas, Barbara bought several packets of Sculpy clay and started making Christmas tree ornaments. She had a brainwave, and got me to draw the technical details, such as I knew them, on a piece of paper. The following day we put in the Blanchards' mailbox a small, colorful replica of Tom in his Carhartt overalls sitting on his lawn tractor, the snowblower attachment spitting small lumps of white clay off to the side.

CURLING

I spend an hour on the landing by the road with a steel shovel, breaking up the ice, which in places is five inches thick, and shoveling it onto the snowbanks. It's nearly forty degrees, and raining. The rain has washed off the snow and polished the ice, and I slide around leaning on the shovel like a tired hockey player leaning on his stick. The chipping itself is not too bad; it's the shoveling that's the strain, gravel clinging to the ice, sand to the gravel, one shovelful weighing as much as ten shovelsful of new snow. Bending, leaning forward and throwing kills my left knee, and more than once I accidentally hit the driveway light with a chunk of ice; the lens is now smashed.

One winter I thought I could get away with just chopping up the ice into fragments the size of my boot, leaving them where they lay, and letting the thaw take care of them, but overnight the temperature dropped thirty degrees and the landing turned into a tank trap. Another year the thaw held, but the meltwater ran off the cleared landing and under the uncleared path down to the house, carving a crevasse twelve inches deep that caught Zoë's foot and nearly broke her ankle. But that's nothing: the same thaw washed out a hundred feet of my friend Lee's driveway, which twists steeply up off Irish Settlement Road in Underhill, facing Mount Mansfield. The damage was so extensive they even got FEMA money to lay down new culverts and repave the driveway. That's a Vermonter's dream: not only the money but the official recognition that things are as tough as we've always said they were. The driveway, now just a well-trodden path through the snow up from the house, is speckled in a fetching shade of dark green. A week ago I dragged the Christmas tree up to the landing for its final and ignominious trip to the dump, and on the way it left final reminders of its visit, which I am loath to clean away.

More freezing rain last night, and this morning the landing was especially treacherous, as a thin, invisible skin of ice covered everything. I felt my Volvo sliding helplessly sideways toward the snowbank as its wheels spun. Luckily I let go in time and ran it back down to the front steps, and more luckily we had a few hand-fuls of salt pellets left. This new ice is hard to crack with the spade, but it's so thin that the salt, with its usual crackling noise, sank straight in and acted like gravel, so at once I could back out and head off into Essex Center for groceries. When I got back I parked on the road, but that's a trick in itself, as everything off the crown of the road is sheer ice—so sheer that when I got out of the driver's side door, having parked a good four or five feet from the edge of the road, I held on to the lip of the car roof and pulled myself along, like human curling.

BLOCK PARTY

After three and a half years, we still felt like outsiders on Chapin Road, so I thought, dammit, we're going to throw a block party. A little after midwinter, just when everyone's feeling that if they don't get out, they'll go insane.

We didn't even know who to invite. The only people we'd ever talked to for more than three sentences were Nick and Bridget Meyer, who own Chapin Orchard, so we asked them to pass the invitation on to anyone who might be interested, and then we stuck fliers in a dozen or so mailboxes on each side of us.

About thirty people turned up, adults crowding upstairs, kids threatening to crush each other on a mini-trampoline under the low ceiling downstairs. We barely recognized any of them; the startling thing was that they barely recognized each other. I'd been assuming that we were newcomers to this semi-rural community, but the fact was, most people hardly knew anyone on the road.

We got a long roll of Maddy's drawing paper, tore off a six-foot section, pinned both ends down with books, drew a rough map of the road, and, for the rest of the party, neighbors bent over it, writing their own names beside their house, adding the names of their children, filling in whatever they could about people who weren't at the party. "I can't believe we've never thought of doing this before," they said.

One set of names we recognized—because it turned up every so often in our mailbox—was Dave and Beth Jillson, who had once owned our house, and, when their family outgrew it, liked Chapin Road so much they built a larger house on the uphill side of the road, a hundred yards or so up toward Westford. The Jillsons turned out to be responsible for everything I liked about the house. It was they who had knocked out a wall and turned the kitchen-dining-room into one large space with modern counters and hardwood floors, made airier by the fact that they had lifted the ceiling and put in sliding glass doors that looked out over a deck, and over the valley. They'd also extended this space by adding the extension that houses the living room and the garage beneath it. But the only thing they talked about was the driveway.

"We hated that driveway," Beth said. "When winter came we just gave up and parked up by the road."

"Every time we drive past now, and see your cars down at the bottom, we shudder," Dave chuckled.

YEAR FIVE

IRIS

Spring comes to Vermont late and fast, as if to make up for lost time, like a competition between bulbs. Tulips are the hip bulb these days, but I'm unmoved by them. The shape of the tulip is too—well, Dutch for me, too solid and well-formed and irreproachable: the comfortable roundness of the bowl, as if designed to fit into the palm of the hand like a brandy snifter, the smooth stiffness of the stem and the leaf and its habit of appearing, all the same height, in a uniform mass. A host of daffodils is far livelier, and daffodils are risk-takers, too, coming up when winter could easily be back, especially around these parts. Snowdrops and crocuses keep a low profile, hugging the ground for cover, but the daffodil throws bulbular caution to the brisk and unpredictable April winds and leaps out of the still-barren winter foliage, nodding emphatically, Yes. *Spring will come, no matter what.* Tulips follow when they're sure it's safe, like schoolmarms with their umbrellas just in case. Tulips take on their color cautiously, too, the head starting green and brightening only gradually, as if to make a bold statement right away were too risky for these Lutheran flowers. Fi-

131

nally they may turn out rich and dark velvet like a Rembrandt, but still they seem a little smug and reserved, like safe sex.

Me, I'm an iris man, the most bohemian of the flowers of our crazed spring. What a fantastic assortment of petals, displayed high and low, this side and that, furled and unfurled like some astounding extravagance in patisserie created for a French courtesan by a pastry chef mad with desire. No telling how many flowers they'll throw out on each sociable stem, nor how many colors to each flower, colors beyond food, beyond paint, in combinations inexhaustible but never clashing. In front of the house, the first thing you see coming down the driveway these days, we have half-a-dozen pale translucent yellow irises peeling out veins of tawny rust like dried blood, and royal Tyrian purple irises breaking into gold and white. There are a thousand others we don't have, some of which win prizes, none of which can be ignored. Bold but delicate, with the faintest downy hairs on the lip like a salacious glimpse offered to a horny bee, the iris, like June in Vermont, is always more than we could have hoped for.

SOMETHING IN NATURE DOES NOT LOVE A LAWN, PART I

It's Memorial Day weekend, and I should be out in the yard like every other American, mowing the knee-deep grass into something approximating a lawn, but I'm not.

In part this is because my old Briggs-powered, no-name gasoline mower, which I bought from the Lawnmower Man in Milford five years ago and haven't serviced since, refuses to start. In part, too, it's because the wet spring is still in full force in Essex Center. While the sandy front yard is dry, the clayey back yard is wet. The dozens of little springs coming up through the back lawn make the whole area look as if it's under attack by an army of moles. Here we are at the end of May, and the soil still squelches underfoot. Mowing would be impossible.

Mostly, though, it's because I'm becoming the world's most hesitant gardener. It's like the tree crisis, only worse. Going out and pulling up anything growing has started to look like a kind of botanical genocide. Why should I have the power to decide that the bird's-foot trefoil should survive, simply because of its yellow flower, while the vetch/spurge/plantain/milkweed/whatever should not?

Mowing is at the industrial end of this slaughter. Every time I get out the mower I hear descriptions of machine-guns mowing people down. I hate to see the bow wave of small creatures scurrying and leaping ahead of the mower. Grasshoppers, crickets, garter snakes, tiny frogs and toads—you just know that some of them don't make it in time. Barbara once mowed a mouse. The swallows in our birdhouses are terrified. They don't mind swooping down on the cats to drive them away, but the mower is clearly a monster beyond their worst imagination: they circle high above the boxes, as if wringing their hands, leaving their offspring to survive this clattering nightmare as best they can. It's perfectly clear: the lawn is an ecosystem, and while Maddy is being taught in preschool to value ecosystems and save the rain forest, I'm playing both God and the angel of death in our back yard.

Historically, lawns were an aristocratic luxury, kept short by sheep. (George Washington, imitating the current English fashions, laid a lawn around Mount Vernon, and grazed it.) The lawn was a green version of the royal carpet, with the additional virtue of demonstrating that the aristocrat—talking of playing God—literally had brought wild Nature to heel.

The little rectangle of grass we are supposed to mow this Memorial Day weekend is largely a suburban twentieth-century innovation, intended to show that everyone could afford his own royal carpet, and everyone could now be master of his own domain. It also had the effect of making a suburb seem unified, so the whole town/subdivision demonstrated a collective conquest of the unexpected, the random, and the dirty. In short, whereas in our dealings with our fellow humans nowadays we stress the value of diversity, in mowing the lawn I'm working for the opposite of diversity, whatever that is. Monolithy. Monotony. Monochromy. Monoculture. Mononymity.

Mowing also does dubious things to the grass itself. If grass plants are clipped before flowers can form, they spread by sending out creepers called stolons and rhizomes, and by tillers, which are small plants that grow from buds that form on nodes on the stem of the mother plant. In this case, though, the grass loses its genetic diversity: every new plant is a clone, vulnerable to the same hazards as its parent. The lawn is growing, but it's not growing: we keep it in a state of suspended evolution.

Mowing reduces the grass's blade area, so the plant loses much of its ability to capture the energy of the sun and photosynthesize it into carbohydrates and sugars. And mowing also harms the grass by reducing the biodiversity of the area. Grass isn't "meant" to grow alone: left on its own, it needs so much water that it's likely to dry out. A healthy area of grass needs other plants such as strawberry clover, yarrow, English daisies, and chamomile.

Not to mention the fact that my mower from the trailer park in Milford was a significant source of pollution. Running a beater of a lawn mower for only an hour releases as much hydrocarbon as driving a car for eleven and a half hours.

So I'm trying out the no-mow lawn. Let it all grow and see what happens. With luck, I'll learn something about biodiversity, about self-sustaining ecosystems. At least I go to bed at night without the sap of innocent plants on my hands.

How is it that I feel ideologically and ethically pure and yet, at the same time, a complete dope?

SOMETHING IN NATURE DOES NOT LOVE A LAWN, PART II

Surprise, surprise: my plan to develop a "natural lawn" is going nowhere.

The results are wonderful if you happen to be a dandelion or a grasshopper, but less appealing if you're a human. The lawn has ceased to be a lawn and has become, in various spots, a meadow, a thicket, a jungle, and a minefield. We've stopped going outdoors. Even the vegetable garden, only thirty feet from the house, seems to be a day's march away, and the sugar-snap peas have started turning scabby on the vine.

There's no mistaking the message: a "natural lawn" is a contradiction in terms unless, like Washington and Jefferson and the English aristocrats they were imitating, you own sheep. As my family can barely take care of a rabbit, sheep seem to be pretty

137

much out of the reckoning, and I've decided to opt for the mower option.

But which mower? I love the stuttering rush-and-retreat of the push mower, like mechanical waves breaking across the lawn, and I like the sense that the effort of mowing reflects, and reminds me of, the effect I'm having on my surroundings. I'd drop from exhaustion long before I did any serious harm to the garden. But those mowers are designed for small lawns that were beaten into submission many generations previously. Ours are large proto-lawns that still have small, gnarly pockets of young sumac, and above the leach field the grass grows dark green, lush, thick and high, reaching cutting length in three or four days.

For the last three years, our yardage was mowed by a neighboring teenager on his father's riding mower, for whom ecosensitivity was less important than listening to music on his headphones. Even if I could afford the lawn tractors and riding mowers that seem to be essential expenditures out here, I've got nowhere to keep it, and like the Briggs it'd just sit on the lower driveway and rust.

For a while I had the use of a non-polluting electric mower, but to cut even a small lawn I had to keep unhooking and paying out cord as I moved away across the grass, and then gathering it up again as I came back. Even so, I invariably got snarled up and ended up mowing the cord.

I really wanted a rechargeable cordless electric mower, but as

138

with most EV technology, I seem to be ahead of the curve: not enough people are prepared to try them for the economies of scale to come into effect, so they start around $500. I was told in confidence that none of the major manufacturers has had much luck with a rechargeable cordless, and the breed is likely to die out. Unfortunately, I spent so long pondering these philosophical issues that by now the grass sneered loftily down at ordinary mowers, and I was forced to go industrial and rent a massive self-propelled mower, at $35 a day.

I'd never used a self-propelling mower, and it turned out to be a very strange piece of machinery. First, it was so heavy I could barely get it into or out of the hatchback. Once it had started, it was very hard to get it to stop. Wrenching at the stiff speed lever, I threw it from neutral straight up to third, and the thing roared off like a metal rhino, grazing a young apple tree and ripping off a strip of bark. An inch farther to the right and the tree would have been snapped in half.

If I had to make a turn it flung me out behind it like a water-skier. It dragged me under a crab-apple, whose lowest branches smacked me across the top of the head and whipped my hat off. Small, tricky areas—I just gave up on them. I tried leaving it in neutral and using it just like a push-mower, but it was so heavy I could hardly shift it. When I took it across the driveway from one front lawn to the other, it sandblasted both my ankles with small stones.

After an hour, my left hand was exhausted from gripping the dead man's handle. I had more or less got the knack of mastering the beast, but if anything, I disliked it even more. Mowing, with this device, became entirely impersonal, merely an act of plodding along behind as it chewed over the ground like a tank. Its unvarying pace suggested a kind of blindness, and of stupidity: it had no idea what was vanishing under it, and it treated everything it destroyed in the same massive, uncomprehending way. By the time I'd finished both front and back, I hated the thing.

Within hours, of course, the lawns needed mowing again. I gave in and got a gasoline mower, albeit one that claimed to be less polluting, and had a neat power-assist that helped me up the near-vertical inclines that make Essex Center somewhat less than suburban.

Now the lawn is a lawn—that is, barely an ecosystem at all— and lies quiet, abandoned by much of its insect population, and the toads and mice have moved elsewhere.

Mostly feel a bit foolish. My anguish, my high ideals, are starting to look absurd, as usual. How on earth could I ever have created a monoculture in this valley? I could mow every day of every summer for twenty years and the lawn would still be mostly clover and dandelions. Nature, once more, has shown herself more than capable of surviving my good intentions.

SAND AND GRAVEL

The head of the driveway is not in good shape. The combination of spring rain and Barbara's habit of accelerating backwards uphill, wheels spitting sandy loam in all directions, have left deep runnels each side of the central hump, and it's only a matter of time before my oil pan or exhaust start scraping the ground.

What I need is another cubic yard of gravel, perhaps two, to level the driveway off, but I can't buy them. I tell myself it's because I don't have a pickup, but it's actually because I'm afraid of the owner of the Hinesburg sand and gravel pit.

It all seemed such an enjoyable project. I wanted gravel for the driveway and sand to make Maddy her own sandbox in the back yard. I'd borrow a pickup and play construction worker for a couple of days.

Over the phone the owner of the pit sounded brusque and impatient. What did I want? Oh, about a cubic yard each of sand and gravel. What? Sand and gravel in the same load? How the heck was I proposing he would do that so the two didn't mix? I hadn't thought of that, and felt pretty stupid. Maybe for the time being

141

I'd just get the sand. That's up to you, he said. We close at five sharp. Better be there.

Vermont being Vermont, all the people I know who own pick-ups are women. Elise had sold her truck, which was perhaps just as well, as the clutch was so stiff you had to stamp on it with both feet, but I could borrow Karen's. I looked at the truck doubtfully. It had an ochre necklace of rust running all round the edge of the bed, and in places daylight shone through holes as big as my hand. I imagined filling it and watching in the rear-view mirror as the sand trickled out all the way back to Essex.

I set Maddy's car seat in the cab and we set off, arriving at the pit a quarter of an hour before it closed. I pulled up to the guard-house. The sentry, who turned out to be the owner, looked at me as if I were the latest in a long series of idiots sent to annoy him.

"We're closed," he snapped.

"But it's not yet five," I said.

"It will be by the time you're done getting your load."

I pleaded with him, which he seemed to enjoy. He was in a time-honored Vermont profession: he owned a bit of the state and was selling it for as much as he could get, to anyone who came along. Eventually he allowed me to pay up front, take a receipt, and drive in to the sand.

I'd never felt so out of place in Vermont—in fact, I didn't feel as if I were in Vermont at all. I once read that the British sci-fi se-

142

ries *Doctor Who* was largely filmed in sand and gravel pits, and I could well believe it. It was a strange, Martian landscape. Once through the gateway, the Vermont green vanished, and I was down to a more elemental level, mountains of beige and gray, or more prosaically what I expect are called #2 gravel and #7 sand. A strange, soft road wound between the huge heaps; it was like driving on tawny carpet. Vast dirty-yellow machines the size of entire factories rumbled here and there, as serious in their purpose as I was trivial in mine.

I followed the owner's directions and found a mountain of sand. Maddy, who was sick of being trapped in the cab, asked to get out and slide down the dunes. There was no sign of anyone coming to help, so I said sure, and for a few moments I was on familiar ground, helping her up the sliding sides of the artificial dune, rolling over the top into a kind of crater, behaving like the kind of New Father the owner would presumably regard as utterly daft.

After ten minutes or so I peered over the lip, to discover to my embarrassment that a bucket loader was waiting for us; it must have stolen up with a stealth remarkable in the earth-moving trade.

"Thought you'd gone," said the driver. He had been called over via walkie-talkie by the owner, had found the empty pickup. . . The long and the short was that the office was now closed, and the owner had gone home—not happily, I gathered. As I'd already paid for my load, though, there was nothing the guy could do but fill me up and throw me out.

He nudged one of his twenty levers and sand cascaded into the truck, which lurched and sank alarmingly. I imagined the entire bed falling through, leaving the pickup like a glass-bottomed boat without the glass.

"Um...that'll do," I called out, leaving yet another guy convinced he was dealing with an imbecile. He'd given me no more than half a yard.

This is why people leave the doctor's office without asking sensible questions; this is why people allow car mechanics to get away with murder. I no longer cared about sand, or money; I just wanted to get out of that strange place without feeling like an even bigger idiot than I already did.

JUNK IN THE YARD

I always vowed never to have one of those rural homes surrounded with junk, but what did I know? Here's a list of things at the foot of the driveway, outside the door of what used to be the garage:

— Two infant-sized collapsible chairs, in plastic and metal, weathered to a urine-yellow from being out on the deck for a year. They went with a collapsible table that I think I bought for Zoë, eight or ten years ago. Destination: the Re-Use Zone shed at the dump.
— The tops of two plastic cat-litter boxes. I've had it with cats. Our house is a factory that turns huge bags of cat litter into wet, stinking clods of clay that we dump on a sandy waste patch out back. The only pet I like is our rabbit. I wish we had no indoor pets at all, just a hedgehog that visited every few days for a saucer of milk. In fact, whenever I think of the cats I *feel* like a hedgehog. Destination: Hell.
— The top half of a very large plastic flowerpot, probably a ten-gallon affair, that must have come with a large shrub

or a small tree. I think it lost its bottom half in an accident with a lawnmower. Ever since — in other words, for at least five months — the top half has lain around near the herb bed looking as if the entire pot has been abandoned so long it has started sinking into the earth, and only the upper rim remains above ground level. Destination: the dump.

—A plastic kitchen, probably by Fisher-Price, that someone bought Zoë when she was a baby. Maddy played with it out on the deck until about three months ago, but the little sink gradually filled with a disconcerting mixture of small toy figures, rainwater, and leaf mold. Looking down into it, I saw tiny drowned faces peering up at me. It's too big to fit into Barbara's car, or mine unless the back is empty. Destination: the Re-Use Zone shed at the dump.

—A hideous rusting empty gray propane gas container. Originally part of the gas grill, it has been empty since before we moved to this house, more than five years ago. We dragged it along with the grill because (a) I didn't know it was empty, (b) I didn't know it was detachable, (c) let's face it, I didn't know anything about gas. It was not until about a month ago that I took a wrench to the fitting and realized I could remove the bottle. I felt stunned. It was a moment in which light seemed to

146

be pouring down over me. I knew it was, on a very small scale, a glimpse of enlightenment, but mostly I felt like a fool. Destination: the gas station and beverage redemption center on Route 15. I shan't replace it. Messing with propane strikes me as one of those arcane country skills outsiders are better off without, like knowing about well pumps or septic systems.

—A very large sheet of landscaping fabric, perhaps sixty feet by four. Was that going to have something to do with the cricket pitch? Destination: the garage, probably. I shall have another daft idea for what to do with it in spring.

—Several fieldstone boulders, the largest perhaps thirty inches long, weighing at least a hundred and fifty pounds. There is a rhythm in my family that I seem unable to abandon. Whenever my parents moved— which they did often—my mother spent the first several months keeping an eye open for attractive stones, which she would often carry home herself. My father would collect the largest in a car or a wheelbarrow, and build a rockery. (At one house he also built a dry-stone wall, perhaps one hundred feet long.) My mother planted the rockery, and then we moved again. I've inherited their love of large rocks, and over the last five years I've built up quite a collection. I have just enough time and energy

147

to move them all to the place where they're going to be a
rockery, or the edging for a flower bed or a walk, and then
a dreadful two-week hiatus always intervenes, some time
in the mad growing season of June, and the next time
I visit them half of them have disappeared under grass
and weeds that I cannot mow because the grass is full of
rocks. Last year I made a heroic effort, found thirty or
forty of my collection, and used them to border the herb
patch, and there they still lie, in a slightly squashed oval,
looking dignified and at peace. The rest lie piled a little
distance away, like a terminal moraine marking the end
of a long-lost glacier, with bird's-foot trefoil steadily encir-
cling them. Destination: another rockery, I suppose.

—One railroad tie, the last of my order. A story much like
the rocks, only even bigger and heavier. This last one lies
across the foot of the driveway; at least it stops unwary
visitors driving onto the herb patch.

—Saddest of all, the corpse of my Norway maple sapling,
planted to block the view of our neighbor's collection of
junk. I'm not sure which galls me more: the death of the
tree, apparently from failure to thrive, or the fact that my
yard is now starting to look like his.

AWD

Two hard frosts in three days, and the road has gone from a playful, rubbery autumn surface (thanks to a little rain and all the apple-picking family SUVs turning into Chapin Orchard) to far more serious stuff. The road is locked solid, the dips are now sharp-edged craters six to nine inches deep. It feels not like dirt but like rock. Hey! We're not joking. This is winter on its way.

The driveway has finally taught me two lessons about owning cars in Vermont: get a used Subaru. My Legacy, even though it has 110,000 miles on it, has tighter suspension than the Volvo; it crashes against the hard lips of these tough, frozen potholes, and I slow down.

When the first real snowfall hits, it traps the Subaru at the bottom of the driveway with thirteen inches of new snow. Just for a laugh, I decide to try backing up without shoveling first, just to see how much the TV ads exaggerate. The car goes straight up—zip!—like that. The wheels don't even slip. *Everything in my life changes.*

MECHANICAL
SLED DOG

The first snow of the year, and it suddenly occurs to me, so suddenly and from such an unlikely distance that it's as if I'm imagining it, that America is full of people who have large garages with remote door openers, who park their vehicles indoors in summer and winter, who wax and Armorall, who get mad at the guy in front whose tires are spitting gravel back at them, inflicting a death of a thousand scratches.

This is true, I know, but it has the eerie patina of a foreign language movie. I think of a car as a kind of mechanical husky, sleeping outdoors in all weathers and loving it.

I'm thinking of buying Barbara one of those remote car starters for Christmas. Get the car warmed up and ready while Maddy is still finishing her breakfast, have most of the snow already melted off the windows when she gets out there, the engine purring like a dog.

ICE SEASON

Lake Champlain is now frozen ten miles clear across to New York, so it's finally official: we're beyond winter, and into ice season.

Vermont has an entire catalog of ice, a sociology of ice, an Olympics of ice, a gallery of ice. The first time I saw ice chunks piling up like glazed rubble on the frozen White River it seemed as if the winter here must have ice to spare—and yet the same phenomenon, almost, occurs to mark the advent of spring, when the sheet ice breaks and shifts, and within one morning the low-lying fields on both sides of the Winooski are suddenly strewn and stacked with foot-thick floes, too many to count, too heavy to move, agriculture clearly having to wait for a thaw before last year's corn stubble is even visible. And where the banks are lined with a fringe of alders, the ice seems to have assaulted the bank, tipped up on end and resting against trees, or snapping the smaller trunks sideways. Winter was here, the ice says, and even though the snow may come back time and again through March and April, once the ice has left the snow seems merely petulant.

Ice underlines winter, in literal ways. The first heavy snowfall always has a celebratory and decorative quality; we can't yet take the season seriously. Even the first driveway shoveling seems half a lark. But as soon as I've driven up and down a few times over the snow, and we've tramped up the white steps to the front door, we've packed the snow into ice. Now the more serious menace of winter is just starting to make itself known, albeit invisibly, as the car whines and fails to make it up to the road, or someone slips on the front steps, which have not yet seemed bad enough to chip clean.

For those who have grown up with the ice, of course, it becomes as much an opportunity as a threat. The driveway becomes a sledding route, and on a good icy day it's possible to start at the road, pick up speed down past the spruce and the lilac, steer frantically around in front of the garage, peel hard right to the top of the garden steps, and then it's a clear shot straight down the lawn into the meadow. One windy day, with the snow glazed with ice like a gateau glazed with melted sugar, Maddy made it all the way down to the forest, more than two hundred yards away.

The lake acquires a different dimension, and a different direction: it suddenly becomes what it was in the nineteenth century, not a divide between New York and Vermont but a bridge. The ice fishermen are trudging out there or hauling out their shanties behind an ATV, the paradox being that while ice fishing seems to be the pursuit of the inaccessible, the fish are actually that much

152

closer and more available once the lake becomes something you can walk on. Ice is a blue-collar land grant. The locals drag-racing on Mallett's Bay have come into their own piece of property at last, as they do every winter. I recently heard of a guy who taught his son to drive on the lake, point being that he'd learn to be delicate with the brake, and when he was learning to balance clutch and gas pedal no amount of overrevving would cause him to bunny-leap and stall, bunny-leap and stall like the rest of us did when we started out.

Last week we also had ice art, in a striking and unusual coup by some creative UVM student. The campus theater, having nice sloping roofs and housing the campus heating system, always generates the most spectacular icicles, a barbed and glittering fringe up to ten feet long, lethal to anyone below. Some genius noticed that the UVM sculpture mascot, a bronze catamount, stands maybe fifteen feet from the wall of the theater, and he put two and two together to make about fifty: we were treated to the spectacular and hilarious sight of a punk catamount, the artist having snapped off a dozen large icicles, inverted them, and stuck them down the animal's spine, making the cat look as if it had spiked up its own fur with gel on the way to a Blink-182 concert.

Might as well make use of the ice, I imagine an old-timer saying, 'cos we sure as heck can't get away from it. For me, it's all summed up by a sight I saw in a small bay on the Milton shore in the spring of 1976. The ice had just gone off the lake, and in the lee curve of the bay a billion tiny fragments of ice bobbed and dipped at the very edge of the water, tinkling like a chandelier in a light breeze. I thought I'd never heard a more enchanting sound; but as I looked across to the right, where the breeze struck the shore, I saw that a summer house, imprudently built right above the waterline, had stood right in the path of the floe ice as it was driven by the wind. I scrambled over the vast, dirty slabs on the front porch and saw ice piled up head-high in the dark living room. Against the far wall leaned the grayish winter shell of a small cherry tree. The ice had uprooted it, shoved it through the front wall of the house, and left it there, a reminder for the summer occupants that, in their absence, winter had come and gone.

YEAR SIX

DROVER'S TRACK

The wet spring and summer have given our driveway the contours of an old drover's track over the Welsh hills. Goldenrod has sprouted all down one side, and the weeds thump and rustle against the underside of the car as I roll down to stop. The two tire tracks look like the beds of small rivers, littered with pebbles and large fragments of gravel, and grass grows on the hump between them like rivergrass. Farther down toward the house they become shallower, less distinct, and more erratic, making sharper turns. When Barbara reverses up the driveway her tailpipe, which must be a little lower than mine, scrapes the hump of the drive and gouges a two-foot-long scrape of sand and gravel, the exposed soil a little rawer and less dull than what lies on either side. It seems almost edible, like crumbs of a seedcake.

It seems to be returning to a natural state, insofar as anything regularly driven over by two cars can be natural. To call it a driveway is starting to look like a false distinction. Grass, bird's-foot trefoil, clover, and a dozen other weeds crowd the garage door, the artemisia I planted beside the house is racing outward and now, at the end of summer, sags outward, just reaching the front passenger's-side tire of the car parked outside the house, like a rugby player reaching out to touch the ball down over the goal line with the last of his strength.

The only patch I put much work into is the former apron in front of the garage, once an herb bed, now my strawberry patch. I dug the area up while Barbara was at work, meaning to surprise her, moved rocks, brought in wood edging, broke three clumps of strawberry plants into a dozen plantings, and by the time she came home we had a little plot, a dabbler's kitchen garden. With a row of basil, too, after a couple of weeks, and then lavender.

All these impulsive gardening flourishes will probably turn out to be hasty and ill-advised, like most of my efforts, but they've had their effect: the first car down the driveway now parks outside the front door, and immediately beyond it, in the undefined space before the strawberry bed, the driveway starts looking like one of the abandoned railway beds my family used to hike in England: rocky, level, sunny, speckled with wildflowers.

My energy and enthusiasm ran out fast, and I left the uprooted weeds lying on the driveway. Yesterday was hot, and by this morning the vegetation has passed through limp to flat, as if the third dimension were life itself, and vice versa. I step on it on my way to the car, to the mailbox. By the end of the week it will be part of the driveway.

ORCHARD FOR SALE

Maddy learned to ride a two-wheeler later than many kids. The driveway, of course, was impossible, and we had to haul her bike to the top; but the road itself was more than enough of a challenge, consisting at best of a broken wavy line of smooth streaks interrupted every few yards by potholes and loose chunks of rock and gravel. It took a lot to coax her onto the saddle, and one of the incentives was that we'd go nine houses—that is, about half a mile—down the road to Chapin Orchard.

The Alder Valley was one of the first areas of Essex to be settled, two centuries ago, and Chapin Road was one of the first two roads to run up the valley, safely above the high-water contour on the eastern side of the brook on the slope of Bixby Hill, toward Westford, the next village north. For more than a century, the homes along the valley were mostly farms, working the glacial soil. As recently as 1940, almost the entire valley was cleared for grazing or haying: an aerial photograph shows that the only trees were a small sugarbush here and there, a thin fringe of trees at the very crest of both ridges, a straggling line of alders at the water's edge.

Little changed until 1957 when International Business Machines opened a large plant five miles away in Essex Junction to make wire contact relays, transistor switches, and calculators and was soon the largest private employer in the state. Between 1960 and 1980, the population of Essex tripled, and in its wake land values exploded: between 1965 and 1985 the town's Grand List value increased seventyfold. Essex was suddenly worth a developer's attention, and houses began to trickle out along the valley, one per three-acre lot, one per ten-acre lot, the land so cheap that it came virtually free with the house. The lots filled in one by one, houses climbed Brigham Hill on the west side and Bixby Hill on the east; then suddenly, at the south end, the Essex Junction end, where town water and sewer reached and stopped, five-acre and ten-acre lots, half-a-dozen of them, were abruptly bulldozed, sewered, built and paved, like a strange concrete shrub in time-lapse motion bursting here! then here! into flower, the cow pastures vanishing as if they had never existed, the hillside trees nibbled back in unnatural rectangular geometries, the meadows by the brook carved out in squares and trapezoids right to the brink where the ground fell abruptly away down to the alders and the water which, for the first time, looked untidy, scrubby, out of place, its naturally meandering geometry snubbed by straight lines and right angles.

The north end of Chapin Road, though, is well into Westford, which is still zoned agricultural in thirty-five-acre lots; the road ends by joining Old Stage Road next to a hardscrabble farm where the fieldstone boulders outnumber the Holsteins.

Paved at one end, dirt at the other, Chapin Road runs between suburbia and Westford, between the past and the present. As such, it is a new kind of settlement, all too common in New England: rural suburbia. Chapin Road is neither a self-sustaining village nor a cluster of farms. I love this valley, but I can't call it a community. Strung out along the road and set back from it, we have no common ground apart from the road itself. We see each other in our cars, but we don't meet because there's nowhere to walk to. No pub, no post office in which to exchange greetings and gossip over a pint or a book of stamps. No park, no library or news agent within walking distance. No rec department field, so we can't stroll down on Saturday mornings to watch the kids play soccer or Little League, or on Thursday evenings to chuckle at the Twilight League softball.

This is the small print on the bargain of commuting: the road that leads to paradise also provides the means of its destruction. By moving out to paradise and then driving back and forth, we turn the road, not the people, into the focus, the artery. The country road—and you can see this still, in dirt roads in farming areas— used to go not from town to town but from farm to farm, typically swerving neatly between farmhouse and barn to cut down on unnecessary hauling, with a colonnade of maples to shade the house and keep the horses cool. Now, as there are no longer wagons to load and unload, the road throws off driveways like the stiff, dead branches of Scotch pines, the houses lying farther and farther back from the road, beyond waving-and-chatting distance, even out of sight. The commuter landscape has the flattened, stylized quality of a map: a house this side, then that side, the identical plots of land running away perpendicular to the road, no more to say.

So this has been the importance of Chapin Orchard: it's the only place on the road we have ever walked to, and the only place where we have ever met people — a role the orchard has been playing for a long time.

The Chapins originally came up from Springfield, Massachusetts, where a statue of "The Pilgrim" is actually of Deacon Samuel, the head of the Chapin line. The last of the Chapins, Barbara and Sylvia, still live on the road.

Ichabod Chapin was the first to come north, to Jericho, the next town east from Essex, in 1786; his grandson, A.F. (Barbara's great-great-grandfather) bought a farm in Essex and moved the family there around 1869. The property deed, dating back before the revolutionary war, declared that all the tall pines on the land were to be saved for the Royal Navy. Both W.F., her great-grandfather, and Claude, her grandfather, served as town clerk; she has kept in her barn their old oak rolltop desk.

The Chapins kept several hundred head of cattle, pigs, chickens, and horses; they made butter and cheese, which won some kind of prize at an exposition in New Orleans, of all places: how on earth did it get that far without spoiling? Around 1930, though, they seem to have recognized the slow, painful demise of the Vermont family dairy farm, and foreseen the need to diversify: her father and uncle bought three hundred trees and started the orchard.

Barbara went away to college, spent some time in Boston, then came back to teach. She still owns a sugarbush up behind her house on Bixby Hill and rents it to a sugarer, and in the Seventies she and her brother planted hundreds of spruces and pines on the hill, much to their father's amusement ("He thought Christmas trees were a joke. He was good enough to sell us the rockiest part of the farm"), as a Christmas tree farm that is now run by Sylvia and her husband, Berg.

After Graton Chapin died in the early Eighties, his widow Jesse sold the orchard to Nick Meyer, a young plant-and-soil-science student at the University of Vermont who had been leasing it, and his wife Bridget. Nick built the orchard up to 1800 trees, but more importantly they made it almost into public property.

Almost as soon as we moved to Chapin Road we walked down there with the girls, first carrying Maddy, then walking with her, then helping her ride her bike. We saw the first lambs of spring in the barn, and we saw the cat's litter of kittens. In winter Nick always invited us to check the hens' roosts to see if there were eggs, and to take any we found. We patted the horse on the nose. Barbara, who is, after all, from New Jersey, patted a chicken.

In spring the schoolchildren came from twenty or thirty miles away to see the new lambs and learn about bee pollination. Over the summer Bridget helped teach art classes in the barn; as the apples ripened the farm hosted five school field trips a day for a month, over a hundred children at a time swarming through the orchard or peering at the honeycomb under glass in the apple barn, the bees flying in from the orchard down an enclosed tube and doing their complicated directional dance, as explained by large posters on the walls amid the children's artwork. At the age of thirteen, Nick's daughter Grace and a friend started a theater-camp-cum-drama-group, the Orchard Players, for six- to nine-year-olds, creating their own plays, final production in the barn.

As the apple harvest approached, Nick borrowed rabbits and housed them in cages out by his driveway, turned his few sheep into an outdoor pen, and chased chickens into a run—still more reasons to go there, to get out of the car. We walked down to take a hayride or buy home-made cider, pumpkins, cider doughnuts, chrysanthemums, honey straws, and bizarrely shaped gourds.

We also met our neighbors. Nick and Bridget were giving everyone on the road a destination, and giving the road itself a character that otherwise would have been absent. If ever a farm deserved subsidy, it was this one—not necessarily from the government, who might not be expected to have such good sense, but from us, the residents of the road that gained so much from its active presence.

I did go as far, in June, to call Nick and offer to help him with the harvest if he got swamped, thinking to do my bit in return.

He stopped by to tell me that he wouldn't be taking me up on my offer because he was putting the farm up for sale. He had been involved with it for over twenty years. It was time for a change, and his children weren't interested in taking it over. Time to move on.

And within a week or two we got word that Barbara, needing some retirement income, was planning to break her own portion of the Chapin land—open flat meadow, wooded hillside, sugarbush and hilltop—into several lots and put them up for sale.

The road's future—our future—will be decided, to a large degree, by whoever buys Chapin Orchard. A buyer who understands that farming is not just a business, but has an (almost entirely unrecompensed) aesthetic and social impact for miles around will be a godsend, more than we deserve. Yet who will be surprised if, after a couple of years finding out what hard work apple farming is, he ups and sells it to a developer? And with the new cluster of single-family homes, the road gets paved, the water and sewer lines are extended, and the value of houses like mine actually goes up?

165

CLOUDS

Last summer, when my friends from the San Diego Cricket Club came east to play my own club, the first thing they remarked on was the clouds.

In San Diego, they said, they don't really have clouds. It's either sunny, or the fog rolls in off the ocean. That night, copper-colored fragments scattered across the early evening sky. As the sun fell below Brigham Hill it left a single cloud, just above the ridge, brilliantly etched. The San Diegans stared.

When we heard the first distant booms of the Burlington and Milton fireworks, we trooped out onto the porch and watched the lights flash and flicker off the undersides of the invisible night clouds, like artillery barrages from the next valley.

The following night we had dinner in Essex, New York. As we crossed on the ferry, the cloudline above the Adirondacks included a perfectly sculpted anvil shape, the classic cumulo-nimbus formation soaring to 60,000 feet, promising a thunderstorm. While we waited for our dinner, sitting out on the deck, the clouds thickened, descended, and the first gusts of rain sent us running indoors. The thunder went on for hours: on the way back, the San Diegans stood at the rail of the ferry, staring north and east as muffled flashes glowed inside the clouds and flickered in multiple strikes on hilltops.

They missed the most spectacular clouds of the summer, though. A couple of days later, at the end of another scorching afternoon, my family went over to Mallett's Bay for miniature golf and ice cream. The miniature golf was closed (a strange sight: I expected the astroturf fairways to be overgrown and ragged, but instead only the windmill was down. It was like a disaster at a model railway), but they were still selling ice cream. As we licked our cones, a strange sight began to accumulate over the trees on Marble Island to the west. A perfectly straight line of deep purple clouds was making its way rapidly toward us. Above it was the brilliant powder-blue of a late summer afternoon; beneath it was night.

The clouds made me uneasy—I'd seen something very like this before. Ten years ago, walking across the campus of a local college where I was teaching, I noticed the same fast, dark, low cloud line, as straight as if it had been ruled diagonally from horizon to horizon. As I crossed onto the faculty parking lot it was still some way off; by the time I reached my car it was directly overhead, and unlike anything I'd ever seen. The floor of the cloud wasn't ragged, like raincloud, or soft like lowering mist; it was made up of hundreds of small knotted vortices, alive and boiling. It seethed over-head; it was impossible to believe that the clouds themselves weren't making some kind of angry muttering, and all that could be heard was the ground wind, picking up sharply as the temper-ature dropped by twenty degrees in five minutes. Something was on its way; I got into my car and drove home with my shoulders hunched. Even though I'd never seen anything like it before, it came as no surprise to find out that minutes later, three tornadoes came ashore in Colchester, threw a massive maple through a house on Appletree Point, and picked up a car in Williston and spun it around, the terrified driver still in it.

"You know, I think we might want to finish our ice creams and head home," I said. The cloud line was now almost overhead, and we could clearly see its strangest feature: running along under-neath its leading edge, side to side, was something that looked like a charcoal-colored hedge, ragged but dense and thick, projecting down to within a few hundred feet of the ground. I bundled the kids into the car and we ran east underneath the storm front. When we had straight road, we kept ahead, but as soon as we had to pause or turn it gained on us. The hedge loomed over us, black on purple. I turned on the radio, not telling anyone I wanted to keep an ear open for tornado warnings—not knowing whether we even have the emergency alert equipment in Vermont, or whether the only alert is the neighbor yelling inaudibly above the wind and pointing in alarm.

We raced out to Essex, turned north, and at once the wind leaped out at us, bending trees almost horizontally. In five minutes, night had fallen. I turned on my headlights. Branches snapped, flew into our lights and vanished across the road. The radio crackled and went off the air. As we ran up the lee of Brigham Hill, I tried to remember if tornadoes jump when they reach a crest, and if so, how far. The wind fell abruptly, then lashed out again, then equally suddenly fell silent.

We rolled down the driveway in a strange, indigo calm. "Let's get inside," I said, undoing seat belts and infant seat restraints, half-expecting the sudden bolt of lightning that would split the silence and darkness right over our heads. Barbara and the girls ran in; I followed, taking the three front steps in one stride.

And that was it. It stayed dark. Every few minutes the wind thrashed the trees around the house, then died. The power went out, then came back on. After a while it was merely night, and, shaken and exhilarated, we went to bed.

SCORPION

High ragweed season, and everyone in the house, even Maddy, is sniffing and sneezing. Maddy showed the first signs of strong allergies: the skin under her chin itched, her eyes watered, and she could barely sleep for sneezing and dripping from her nose. She coughed on and off, and I was worried that she might be starting asthma. Zoë suffered too, though for her it also felt like a sore throat. Barbara developed a sinus headache that refused to budge, like a bird's nest wedged in a chimney. My own asthma came back as a slight rasp in the evening, and I thought of moving back to Burlington — how stupid, to buy a house in the middle of an entire valley of grasses and weeds! — and of what that would cost us.

One afternoon I roamed around the house with a pair of clippers and cut down every ragweed plant I could find, holding my breath as if it could emit spores of anthrax. It gave me little satisfaction and did no good, of course. I was horrified to see how much I'd neglected the driveway and the small plots of garden around it. My show-bed beside the front door, the little triangle that catches all the warmth of the southern sun and is sheltered from the wind by the house, was all tangled. The rhododendrons were vanishing behind a rising hedge of clover, the lilies had been infiltrated by milkweed, the creeping phlox was not to be seen, and on the drive-way side of the railway tie that is my poor man's landscaping timber grew a thicket of ragweed, fourteen inches tall, leaping out of the compacted gravel of the driveway as if to prove its meanness: *This is how tough I am. I scorn your composted topsoil, your sheltered nook. I am a scorpion of a plant. I will grow anywhere.*

FALLING APART

The first hard frost fell last night, the meadow and lawn crisp and gray as far up as the swing set, and the front lawns as well. Two of the ash trees, the one outside my office window and the one at the head of the driveway, have clearly been triggered by the change of season and are melting leaves. Before I started the car, parked in the landing at the top of the driveway, Maddy and I sat and listened to the steady, almost continuous patter and rustle of the leaves falling through the branches, and the light metallic taps as some landed on the roof of the car.

The tree was falling apart. The leaves were falling almost more quickly than I could count them: twelve seconds on my watch, and I counted thirty-three gone, twisting and landing on the driveway, the road and the soft earth of the car bay.

As I walked back down to the house, I saw a distinct but strange pawprint in the soft gravel of the driveway and bent over it, puzzled. Then laughed—it wasn't an animal track at all. Yesterday afternoon I went to watch Zoë play soccer at Brown's River Middle School in Underhill, an epic game that Zoë's school won against a better team. When we got home and walked together down to the house, she must still have been wearing her cleats.

By the following morning, when the cold snap had passed and the heart of the valley was hazy with a veil of morning mist, the ash tree at the head of the drive had lost perhaps seven-eighths of its leaves. Half or more of the branches were completely naked. None of the other ashes—and we have half a dozen—is so far gone. Maybe it's the effect of being so close to the road that has weakened it.

The grader has been past a couple of times, and the driveway, instead of meeting the road on the same level, as if both were part of the same universal gravel transportation plan, now rushes and debouches out and down onto it, for the road is a full inch and a half lower than the head of the drive.

This has the twin effect of making both seem illegitimate, or at least damaged. The drive is no longer part of the road, the line of demarcation now perfectly clear. The road has its own purpose and trajectory, and rushes past like a stationary torrent; the driveway is merely an add-on. And it's true, the road is far older than the driveway, probably a century older, perhaps a lot more. But now at last it's clear what regular and heroic maintenance keeps the road together, what large, heavy machinery, its pawprint evident in that straight cutoff line, grooms the road to its (mostly) satisfactory flatness and hardness.

173

Yet that flatness and hardness are, of course, the products of a kind of artificial erosion. Scraped and packed by the grader in summer, scraped and packed by the plow and the sand truck in winter, the maintenance of a dirt road is almost a tidal occurrence, but in the end the road is creeping and trickling just one way: down.

For lack of anything better, I'll probably go up there with a spade and take off that edge, scattering the inch and a half of loam across the road like a token offering of thanks, a small reimbursement, to make the join seem smooth once more, to make it seem as if nothing really is changing and the valley is not, in this half-inch-by-half-inch fashion, filling back up.

CRUNCH

"Crunch, crunch, crunch, crunch," goes the song Maddy has learned in kindergarten, "that's the season's cheer!"

And it is. Spring is a spectator season, therefore an adult season, except that at last you get let outdoors. Summer—well, we talk of soaking up the rays, but that's still pretty sophisticated, to build an active pleasure out of a passive posture. No, the seasons that work are the participant seasons, autumn with its crunch, the sound that you are making an impact and it is responding, rake the leaves and jump into the pile. And winter even more so, of course, shaped in the hand, flung at the friend, the sister, the passing car.

FOSSIL LEAVES

Last Sunday, Barbara dropped me off on Colonel Page Road and I walked home, taking a shortcut that followed a deer track through the rough growth up to Chapin Road. The recent weather, a very wet day followed by two dry ones, has created a remarkable texture in the road. The leaves are now in full fall, and every few inches one had fallen while the road was wet and soft, had stuck, but had not yet been obliterated by passing cars. As a result, the whole putty-colored surface of the road looks like a large, flat stone that an archaeologist has broken open along a sedimentary fault to reveal perfectly-preserved fossils. The leaves have barely a trace of their original colors or contours, and are now pressed into the uppermost surface of the road, but their outlines and veins are still perfectly intact, and in many cases the quarter-inch or so of stem has enough spring to curve upward, as if refusing to leave its natural element, the air.

The fossil leaves are a remarkable sight, so perfect and delicate, yet no longer themselves. They are exactly midway between being part of the tree and part of the road.

STICK SEASON

The old Vermont name for this time of year, the gray-brown November pause between fall and serious snow, is "stick season," according to my friend Ev Grimes, who has interviewed countless Vermonters for the Vermont Folklife Center. As soon as she said that, the name made sense. In part it's because there are simply a lot of sticks about, blown down by the recent high winds. But I take the phrase to mean something deeper and grimmer. "Stick" implies wood that is dead, motionless, detached, and that's how the entire landscape seems now that we have been dealt the real cards of winter. The trees themselves have become sticks.

I first noticed this three weeks ago when I bought a bow saw and did some shaping of the ash tree in our back yard that was blocking half our view of the valley. The temperature was down to perhaps fifteen degrees, and even before the saw finished its cut, the last sliver snapped sharply, and the leafless branch fell to the frozen ground with a rattle.

In summer, the gentle stirring of trees is profoundly reassuring; it suggests that long after I'm gone there will still and always be a gentle movement—a life, a sense of purpose—through all things. The wind is an invisible benediction.

Not now, though. Woodsmoke is snatched sideways from the mouths of chimneys, but the trees, with no leaves to catch the wind, offer at best a stiff, edgy side-to-side shifting, resentful, wanting to seize up beyond all memory of life, no more than a bundle of sticks.

SUBURBAN
PERMAFROST

Two cold days, a light overnight snowfall, and the gravel already feels different underfoot: crisper, rougher. I suppose the moisture in the fines has frozen. The top crumbles, but underneath it's solid, as if incorporated into the bedrock. I hadn't thought to notice how much give there usually is in gravel. Now it's suburban permafrost.

CARPET OF ICE

The driveway has really upped the ante on us. We were doing well for a while this winter, until about two weeks ago when it rained.

It rained for almost a whole day. The rain washed away the snow, leaving exposed ice everywhere, then froze onto the ice. The driveway became a transparency of its former self: the ruts in the snow turned into ruts in ice that trapped my wheels, ruts that were three inches of solid ice in the trough and six to eight inches thick at the crest.

At first I thought I was being clever: I discovered the remains of the Shur-Pac, which I'd bought to fill in the ravines caused by the fall rains, buried under a foot of snow up by the parking bay, and I threw shovelful after shovelful down the driveway, watching the fragments of rock and pellets of loam bounce and roll downhill until they found a dip to lodge in. Four cubic feet ended up on the ice, reddish-brown patches like stains on the immaculate surface, and they did their job: Barbara could get out of the parking bay at the top, and the Subaru, always a trooper, reversed up the driveway with barely a slip, the only problem being the ruts, which kept threatening to steer me off into the spruce halfway up the slope.

180

So all was dandy until two days ago, when we had a day of thaw, forty degrees and the sound of dripping from the eaves all day and night, and then another dip. Yesterday the wind picked up, blowing the dusting of fresh snow off the driveway, and everything froze solid again. Getting up and down was no longer a game, or even a challenge: it was a danger.

"But I *like* ice-skating," Maddy protested, happily slipping and sliding her boots back and forth as her body stayed in place, padded in her snowsuit, her center of gravity enviably low to the ground. She wasn't the one carrying the groceries.

This morning the thermometer read eleven below. For the first time, the Subaru almost didn't make it out. I sat there at the bottom going nowhere at all, and only got any traction by ramming forward into the snowbank so my front wheels were on fresh terrain, then backing out smartly. Three times I slid sideways toward the waiting embrace of the spruce; three times I had to go back down and ram into the bottom snowbank again.

When I finally clawed my way out, the tires miraculously finding purchase on sheer ice a Zamboni would have been proud of, I thought the day's troubles were over. They had barely begun.

I dropped Maddy off at school, and went back home: we had called a carpet cleaner, who was due at 10 a.m., and I had to clear the living room of furniture and 14,201 tiny utensils, items of kitchenware and small figures from Maddy's doll's house, then vacuum up several dozen of the small dried pellets that the rabbit leaves anywhere that reminds him of a burrow. Then, once the carpet was dried, I had to put everything back, as it was Maddy's birthday and everything needed to be set up for her party. We'd been through all this upheaval once before and then forgotten to be home when the carpet cleaner arrived, and he had just turned round and left. I was damned if I wanted to go through it yet again. Today would be Clean Carpet day.

I parked in the bay at the head of the driveway and started to pick my way cautiously downhill.

As soon as I left the flat of the parking landing and took a step downhill I knew I was in trouble. The day's thaw had let the Shur-Pac sink into the ice, which had then frozen again above it, leaving it looking like a swarm of gritty insects trapped in white amber. Stepping on the thin remnants of snow did no good. My right foot began to slide, I took half a step to try to get my balance, and next instant I was gone, hitting the ice *hard* with my right hip, right elbow, and the heel of my right hand, jarring my neck, leaving my head ringing.

I struggled to my feet and made it down to the house, nearly falling twice more, thinking again what a miracle the Subaru was to get up when I couldn't even get down. Then I remembered the carpet guy.

At once I imagined myself in a court of law, the judge scowling at me. If I had invited the carpet guy, he was saying, it was my responsibility to make the driveway safe for him. Had I done so? Well. . . . I scattered fifty pounds of Winter-Melt, hearing the constant faint crackling of the ice as it went to work, stepping in the tiny pockmarks it made. The judge was not impressed. I took the spade and inched up and down again, chipping a line of caterpillar-track grooves in the ice. Hmmm, said the judge.

I went inside, picked up the 14,201 tiny utensils and vacuumed the rabbit pellets by 10 a.m. No sign of the carpet guy. I called the company. "He got frozen in at his last job," said the boss. "Those vans have got no traction at all." Thinking of the judge, I told him about our driveway. "Have you got any sand? If so, you could try sanding and I'll send him on over." I'll give it a try, I said, crept back up the driveway and discovered that the Shur-Pac was frozen solid. I couldn't chip it with the spade. I couldn't chip it with a hammer.

The mail carrier arrived, we commiserated, and she handed me our mail through her window. I couldn't understand why it was wet—until I discovered that the fall had cut open the heel of my right hand, and blood had spread across my wrist and was running across the letters.

I picked my way from one melting spot to another down our mockery of a driveway, took off my boots, threw them in a corner, and called the carpet guy to postpone. Again.

Two nights later, I came home from playing indoor soccer and it was raining. Didn't even bother trying to drive down to the house; wedged my car in as close behind Barbara's as possible, hoping it wasn't sticking out into the road. Couldn't imagine the plough being out that night anyway.

It was very dark at the head of the driveway—the light has been buried for weeks—but I could make out the ice gleaming all the way down. This was ludicrous. There was no way I could walk down, or even make it across to the sides of the driveway. I sat down, thinking I'd just slide down on my backside, and edged myself toward the crest with my heels. At once I shot off downhill so fast I fell backwards, and that was how I arrived home, lying on my back, my gym bag in one hand, soaked from my jeans to the hair on the back of my head, laughing like an idiot. You can't do that in San Diego.

YEAR SEVEN

MYSTERY BIRD

Something utterly unexpected happened when we moved here: I became a bird-watcher. It has something to do with winter: anything that moves or makes a sound out in the frigid valley deserves all the sunflower seed it can eat.

This is a wonderful spot for birds. Being on the side of a long shallow valley, with a dense little knot of pines beside the house and an open meadow falling away to the valley floor, we get open-field species, and edge species, and thicket species: bluejays, chickadees, cardinals, redcap sparrows and juncos in the winter, red-winged blackbirds, hummingbirds, pine grosbeaks, grackles, pileated woodpeckers, goldfinches, robins, swallows and tufted titmice in the summer. And down in the forest, owls, hawks, and wild turkeys.

Either the first or the second summer I began noticing what we called either The Mystery Bird or The Laughing Bird. The first name we gave it, I'm pretty sure, was The Mystery Bird, because we never saw it. Every so often, most frequently around dusk, I'd be walking up the driveway on my way to weed the vegetable garden and I'd hear its distinctive call, sounding so close above our heads I'd duck—but when I looked up I never saw anything. Thus it also became the Laughing Bird, partly because its call sounds vaguely like a laugh, and partly because it seemed to be laughing at my inability to see it.

I'd never heard a bird anything like it. The call was better imitated than described, but it sounded like someone blowing across the top of a small bottle—skillfully enough to produce a clear, if breathy, note—between eight and fifteen times in very quick succession. Or perhaps blowing into a very breathy slide whistle, because most of the time the notes rose in pitch over a range of about three full tones, with the last couple of notes sometimes falling off a little.

This sequence would be repeated several times: we'd hear it somewhere not far to the south, then shortly afterwards right over our heads (again the involuntary flinch, the startled look upwards, the empty sky), then a little way to, say, the northeast. It often seemed to be circling our house in a large loop—or maybe that was just a kind of paranoia brought on by this musical strafing by an invisible bird.

After about three years, I finally saw the Mystery Bird, and I realized at once why I'd never seen it before. It was flying much higher than it sounded—not quite as high as a lark, perhaps, but a lot higher than the swallows, grackles, blackbirds, and robins that hop around at or below treetop height—and it was making a much louder call than you'd think. Once I caught sight of it and held on, hardly daring to believe my luck, I noticed that it also had a distinctive and odd flight pattern. As we'd thought, it flew in a large loop, but it did so in a roller-coaster fashion, beating up to a peak, falling, beating up again.

Now that I knew where to look I was able to watch it several times a summer, but it still had its mysteries. For one thing, it was always solitary. For all I know it might be the only one of its species in the valley, or in the world. For another, nobody who visited our house and was finally able to spot it had heard anything like it, either. Oh, and one other thing about its call: I couldn't figure out why it did it. It wasn't a flocking call or a roosting call. If it was a mating call it was singularly unsuccessful, as I only ever saw the one bird, and unless it was catching high-altitude insects it wasn't a feeding call.

I used the word "beating" to describe its motion because it was not a graceful bird. It flew rather like a duck, as if flying took virtually all its energy, its wing-beats as rapid as any largeish bird I've seen. It was shaped a bit like a duck, too, only with a shorter neck, and it didn't have a duck's level, purposeful flight. I couldn't tell you what color it is: as I most often saw it at dusk, and at a considerable altitude, it was either dark against the sky or brilliant as the sun caught it. Not much help there. Oh, and the wings were a

189

rather odd, scimitar shape: seen from directly below, they curved forward and then tapered back. Not broad wings, either: they seemed a little short for its body weight, which might explain why it beat them so quickly.

One final odd thing: it flew, apparently, all day and night. It was one of the bird's wonderfully mysterious qualities that if I woke up in the middle of the night and gazed out of the bedroom window in the moonlight, I'd likely as not hear it laughing and echoing invisibly overhead in the darkness, the genie of the valley.

"Ideally, bird-watching gives you both [a] symbol and a living bird," wrote Jonathan Rosen in the *New Yorker* that arrived last Tuesday. "You bring along a guidebook, an artifact of the literary world, even as you wander out into nature in pursuit of something wild. You experience the thrill of seeing an untamed creature, but immediately you cage it in its common or scientific name and link the bird—and yourself—to a Linnaean system of nomenclature that harks back to the Enlightenment notion that nature can be ordered. And behind Linnaeus lurks the Biblical belief that, like Adam and Eve, we have always named animals; it is our job."

Reading that passage, I made my mistake. Thinking that I'd settle this mystery once and for all, I emailed a bird expert I know who lives on one of the islands in Lake Champlain, describing the bird in fascinated detail, enumerating its odd characteristics as much to myself as to him.

He emailed back right away. It's a common snipe, he said. The characteristic sound is called "winnowing"—the snipe makes it with its slotted outer tail feathers.

That night, for some reason, I couldn't sleep. Hour after hour I heard the winnowing circle and recede—but instead of being mysterious, it was now common. By 4 a.m. I found myself thinking "Bloody snipe!"—a sentence I couldn't have conceived before.

To hell with Linnaeus. Some things are better not named, are better left to circle and hoot softly in the darkness of the imagination.

When a robin right next to the house took over at 4:30 a.m., drowning out the snipe, it was a relief.

A RIDICULOUSLY
SHARP TURN

Today we had the Jillsons over for lunch; they have become friends, and Beth is now Zoë and Maddy's pediatrician. They wandered round the house, gazing affectionately here and inquisitively there at the changes they made to the house, and at how those changes have changed.

Dave Jillson told me the tragedy of the garage. After they had built the garage/living-room extension, they found (as we did, too) that the newly finished garage was virtually useless: to get into or out of the garage took such a sharp turn, and the level, graveled apron outside the garage was so small, that it always took them half-a-dozen tries to get out of the garage and around the corner so they were facing up the driveway. The driveway had defeated the garage, they realized: they'd just built what amounted to a very expensive storage shed.

The astonishing thing, though, was what he added as an afterthought. Before they built the extension, he said, the driveway ran all the way round to the back of the house; what is now Zoë's bedroom was the garage. I stared at him, and we both went out onto the deck to consider this. The driveway must have been shaped like a flattened question mark. The driver must have had to make a turn that was ridiculously sharp, a full 180-degree U-turn within ten or twelve feet, and then elbow his way into a tiny space barely larger than a Yugo. We shook our heads. Who on earth would design a house like that? It confirmed what I'd always suspected: that our driveway had never been a functional conduit; it had never suited the needs of the automobile age.

The more I thought about this, the more I liked it. Vermont houses never used to have driveways. Farms were built astride the road, house on one side, barn on the other, a line of maples out front to shade the horses — no driveway at all. Why would you want to haul things to and from the road any farther than absolutely necessary? The long, baronial driveway of recent years, cutting through the front field to a grand house set way back from the road, is just another occasion to pave over several thousand square feet of farmland, to become a back-to-the-land suburbanite with a minivan. I was glad to have a driveway that was short, steep, and difficult. Ridiculous, even.

BASIC WIRING

As part of my lifelong application process to become a Vermonter, I'm teaching myself to sheetrock. I thought I'd start by finishing a closet down in Barbara's sewing area.

You have to understand, it was pretty much a junk space beforehand, a gap under the stairs into which someone had nailed some two-by-fours and some sheets of plywood to create shelving, and then put a couple of doors on the front, whose thumb-latches gave them an especially rustic feel. It was painted Vermont barn red, and had immediately signaled to us that it was no more than a dumping ground—and sure enough, it had immediately attracted a thousand odds and ends that would have been better thrown away. So it remained for five years until early November, when Barbara was bemoaning the lack of shelf space in that area of the den. It didn't seem especially ambitious of me to decide to rip out plywood and two-by-fours, nail sheetrock up over the studs, throw on a couple of coats of paint and then some decent pine shelving, preferably horizontal.

Frankly, I might be a lot farther along if I hadn't decided to teach myself wiring at the same time.

I've never wired anything, being petrified of fire or electrocution, but in putting up the sheetrock I found a wire in the wall,
leading to the switch that turns on the ceiling light. Aha, I
thought. The room was chronically short of outlets; I would run a
wire (I was pretty sure this was the right phrase) from the switch
down a couple of feet and put in an outlet, a brave little extension
I thought of as the Outlet Hyperlink.

Little did I know that I would never be in the slightest danger
of death by fire or electrocution, but that I was in just about every
other danger, and by the end of the day a bit of electrocution
would have seemed like comic relief.

When I presented myself as the paragon of ignorance, the guy
at Aubuchon not only picked out the bits and pieces I'd need, he
also found a scrap of paper and kindly drew me a diagram. Like
many diagrams, it made sense as he explained it, but later seemed
to suggest that I should have two white wires and three black wires,
which I was fairly sure wouldn't be a good idea, especially as the
extra black wire seemed to go sideways out of the switch — into the
sheetrock, perhaps, or the insulation.

My mother always said that if you get a book from the library,
you can do anything, so I borrowed a book called *Basic Wiring*,
waited until the girls were off making stained-glass tree ornaments, found the right circuit and turned it off, pulled out the
switch, and started stripping insulation like a Frenchman butter-
ing a baguette. I was thoughtful, I was methodical, I referred reg-

195

ularly to *Basic Wiring*, and I didn't come even close to electrocuting myself. In no more than forty-five minutes I had the outlet wired. I plugged a small desk lamp into the outlet to act as a circuit tester, and I threw the breaker.

The desk lamp went on—Eureka!—but the room otherwise seemed oddly dark. Why was that? Hmmmm. Then I realized: the outlet worked, but now the ceiling light didn't.

I checked my diagrams carefully. I had done just what the book said. I called my friend Bill, who owns a recording studio and is constantly plugging things in here and there. Bill was equally puzzled. The only explanation that I could come up with to fit all the facts was that the electricity, having gone downwards through the ordeal of the switch and the gauntlet of the outlet, was so exhausted that it couldn't face the prospect of climbing all the way back up to the light again.

Bill wasn't convinced by the tired-electricity theory. What I should have done, he said, was break into the cable *before* it reached the switch. That way the wiring of the switch would be unchanged. Made sense to me. It was also sort of like what the guy in Aubuchon had advised. Right.

I broke into the cable above the switch, split it open with a casual savagery that pleased me greatly, separated out the three wires, clipped the white wire first (just to be on the safe side), stripped an inch of insulation off the end of each, brought up the white wire from my Outlet Hyperlink, and tried to wrestle all three bare ends into one tiny little orange plastic cone.

It was like trying to wrestle three piglets into one nightcap. If I tried to jam the cone over the wires, as soon as I let it go to reach for the electrical tape, the cap would ping off and land between my feet in a slowly-growing pile of debris, mostly small black twists of electrical tape pulled off and hurled to the floor in fury. If, on the other hand, I tried to tape at the same time as I shoved the cap over the exposed copper ends, one of them would hastily back out like the aforementioned piglet, and after a minute's forceful taping I'd realize I had connected only two of the wires, and the third was somewhere else entirely. Then I had to strip all the tape off the cap and try again.

All this taping created another hazard, I realized. I was cutting the tape from the roll with my utility knife, and at one point I looked down at what I was doing and noticed that I was trying to hold the switch box, the incoming cable, the Outlet Hyperlink, three bare wires, an orange plastic cap, and the free end of the tape all in my left hand, while slashing at the tape with the knife in my right. If I succeeded in cutting the tape, I stood a fighting chance of going straight through the webbing of my left thumb as well.

What you need, I told myself, is better working conditions. So instead of bending down to pick up pliers, tape, screwdriver, and utility knife every time I needed them, I put them on the lintel above my head. Much better. I taped the white wires, I taped the black wires, and as a kind of lap of honor I thought I'd tape the ground wires too, even though I was pretty sure I didn't need to. I reached up for the tape, and all but knocked the utility knife, its blade extended and probably septic with sheetrock dust, off the lintel for it to impale me in the top of my head.

I took a deep breath, stepped carefully out of the closet and let my breath out again slowly. Okay. Okay. I stepped over two tape measures, one hammer, five screwdrivers, two cases of drill bits, a ball of twine, a spirit level, a T-square, two saws, a length of spare cable, an electric drill, an extension cable, a pair of wire cutters, two pairs of pliers, two pencils, an air filter, a box of nails and three packs of screws that had by now been kicked and scattered across the carpet, reached into the panel, and flipped the breaker. The ceiling light went on. Yes! But after a moment's rejoicing I looked down at the desk lamp, which was off. I jiggled the switch both ways with my toe. Nothing. I had fixed the light, but now the outlet didn't work.

I had to pick up the girls in ten minutes. Gritting my teeth, I decided I'd wire the switch back up the original way, throw up my sheetrock, and nobody would ever know of my plans for an outlet. I turned off the current, ripped out all the wires, pulled off the tape, wired the switch back up, stuck it back in the wall, threw on

198

the current and, pulling on a glove, gingerly flicked the switch. Nothing happened. My knees were aching, my arms were itchy with fiberglass, my eyes were strained, and all I had to show for four hours of work was that now nothing worked.

So I have two questions. One: where did I go wrong? And two: am I now farther away from being a Vermonter, or closer?

BASIC WIRING

LEAVE TWO
ENVELOPES

My training to be a Vermonter, having been as painful as might be expected, has come to a temporary halt, as I've finished refinishing the downstairs closet, sheetrock and all. The house is looking even more like a Vermont house, too: stacked up around the foot of the front steps are a dozen boards, a couple of old doors with thumb-latches, and several sheets of unused, soggy, putty-colored sheetrock that got rained on before I had a chance to take them to the dump.

The closet is now brighter, handier, more spacious—more modern, in a word. Yet just before I finished it, I made a discovery that threw a bucket of cold water over my self-satisfaction.

It wasn't until I started pulling the closet apart that I discovered just how ham-fisted a carpentry job it had been. Nails from every angle, ugly unfinished plywood sheets banged in two thick, joints that didn't meet, a few half-fitting rolls of fiberglass insulation. . . .

200

I went to work with a hammer, a crowbar and a good dose of contempt.

Then I pulled out a vertical sheet of plywood and found that a small cache of items had fallen down in the space behind it, and as I looked more closely, I saw that this was, in its modest way, a treasure trove. One woman's dress shoe, white. Some mystery woven textiles — clothing? Mats? A faux-leather briefcase containing some blank paper and calculator tape . . . and two documents.

These were crucial in two respects: they dated the cache, and they identified the house's owners at that time. Both bore the names of the Fischers, who, as far as I know, were the original owners of the house.

One document was an order receipt from Spring Hill Nurseries, made out simply to "Mrs. Bruce Fischer, Chapin Road," a sign that there must have been only a handful of houses on Chapin Road at the time, barely twenty-five years ago. She had spent a fair sum on flowers and plants — Bluechip Campanula, Shasta Daisy Miss Muffet, Russian Olive, Lombardy Poplar — but none of her plantings, apart from a carpet juniper, were still thriving outside. Gardening around here is such a gamble: despite the hard work, all the preparation of the beds, far more than half my own plantings have failed just because I didn't know what I was doing. Maybe she didn't know either; maybe she did, and some later occupant dug them up or neglected them. The air here is so full of seed that it wouldn't take long for the dainty seedlings to be overrun by weeds, the valley's hooligans.

The other document, amazingly, was Bruce Fischer's resume.

He was twenty-five, at six foot two inches almost exactly my height and at two hundred pounds almost exactly my weight. At the time he was working at Vermont ETV, just down the road from Vermont Public Radio, where I worked a decade later. He was an assistant producer, making $9,000 a year after a couple of raises of which he was obviously proud. He had made a Christmas special and an hour-long documentary on the St. Johnsbury and Lamoille County Railroad "on a budget of less than $1 million." (I'm not sure which is more remarkable — that he thought to brag about the fact that the budget was so small, or that ETV could afford a budget that was so large.) His summer job resume included night concession stand manager for the Westbury Music Fair, Maitre d' at Port Authority — what?? — flower delivery boy, and vending machine attendant.

His hobbies, he said, included woodworking, and, in a final line that was printed so far down in the margin it fell half off the bottom of the page, he concluded "I am mechanically inclined and considered a pretty fair carpenter."

A pretty fair carpenter! Yet at that instant, my contempt for him evaporated. He sounded too much like me, this young man keen to get ahead, to appear eager and hardworking, to do his best to get his family out of this little starter home and into something more comfortable, yet transparently in love with Vermont. ("Married: Yes. Relocate: No. Travel: Yes.")

Whatever the reason, the closer I came to finishing, the more my own shortcomings and shortcuts were obvious. I should have added another layer of mud along the joins, making the finish smoother, more seamless. I should have planed one particular spot—but by now I just wanted to get finished, to get out.

I had improved things, yes, but the next generation to own this house would be able to pour as much scorn on my handiwork as I had on poor Fischer's, could entertain plans of installing track lighting, perhaps, or some wireless technologies as yet undreamed of.

I thought of the old Soviet Union joke, in which a new Secretary takes over the eastern Empire on the death of his predecessor, and finds two envelopes on his desk. The first contains a card that says simply, "Denounce me." The second contains an identical card that reads, "Leave two envelopes."

RISK, MORBIDITY,
AND MORTALITY

I don't usually think of the driveway as a place of risk and drama, and I still didn't think in those terms even when Barbara pulled hard off the road and came barrelling downhill just as the rest of us were walking up, and we had to leap aside pretty smartly.

But then I came across "Driveway Injuries in Children: Risk Factors, Morbidity, and Mortality," by Evan P. Nadler, MD; Anita P. Courcoulas, MD; Mary J. Gardner, RN; and Henri R. Ford, MD, an article in *Pediatrics*, August 2001, full of sad, brief references to injuries to "the musculoskeletal organ system," "crush injuries," poor outcomes and deaths, especially to those under two years old, struck by a light truck or SUV going in reverse.

"Injuries that occur around the driveway are not typically regarded as reportable to the police and thus are often underrecognized," the authors say, hinting at our sense that the driveway is not really a road, and therefore not really dangerous, even though designed for lethal weapons weighing two tons.

Nevertheless, over the previous thirteen years, sixty-four children who sustained motor vehicle–related injuries in or around a driveway were admitted to the authors' Level 1 pediatric trauma center. The mean age was 3.37 years.

"Parents of young children must be educated regarding the perils of the driveway," the authors say, wagging the finger, so consider yourself educated. In particular, children should never be left unattended around the driveway, and motor vehicles should be locked (windows and trunk) when left in the driveway; though on the bright side, "It is interesting to note that children who set a vehicle in motion were not as severely injured as those who were struck by vehicles driven by an adult driver."

"Parents should also discourage the use of the driveway as a recreational area," the study concludes. But the driveway is a natural playground. In England, three stumps chalked on the garage door for cricket; in this country, the basketball hoop above the garage. It's a multi-user space; the only problem is that one of the users is a mechanical rhino.

In a sense, we're lucky, our driveway being so primitive, its bounce so uneven. We'll never be out there at dusk, Zoë and I, playing a little one-on-one, when Barbara barrels in from work, eyes tired in the half-light, thinking only of dinner, the chance to put her feet up.

WELL AGAIN

It came back again on New Year's Eve, like a ghastly reminder of time and mortality, like Old Father Time wielding not a scythe but a pipe wrench: we had no water.

Just after darkness fell on December 30th, the shower quit. The taps in the kitchen sink coughed, spat, and stopped. The toilet yielded one last flush. Then we were dry.

My initial fear was that the well had run dry. All up and down our road, wells have been drying up since early summer. Neighbors walking their dogs would stop to shake their heads and say, "That well hasn't run dry in twenty years. . . ." At first it was only those living on the uphill side of the road, and I felt safe; but then one morning our next-door neighbor's house had the now-familiar silhouette of the upturned drill rig. The drilling went on for two days. I forget the exact figures, but the drill went down six or eight hundred feet before they hit water, and the whole bill came to the best part of ten thousand dollars.

So there was a certain tension in the house, broken only when Maddy, nearly seven, dug in her backpack and offered us the water in her plastic water bottle. I called the guys who had installed our new pump only five years back. Nobody could come out until morning, and that night we went to bed anxious and pungent.

The well guys turned up around nine, and I liked them at once. One grunted, the other smoked. Both wore thick Carhartt tan coats, rhino-hide gloves and rhino-skin boots. The leader checked the water level in the well by the old-science method of calling down "Hello?" and then cocking his head for the echo. He did complicated and potentially lethal things with a voltage tester and announced that the problem was at the bottom of the well — either a bad wire or a bad pump.

"So it's as inconvenient as it could possibly be, then?" I asked.

"Did you expect anything else?" he said, with the ghost of a grin.

They turned down the offer of a hot drink and went back out into the cold, heating their rhino-hide gloves with a blowtorch and addressing the wellhead, which poked maybe two feet up out of the snow.

In my ignorant mind, a well was pretty much a cylinder full of water, such as you might drop a bucket into, only narrower. The first thing the guys extracted, though, was a thicket of wires, and then, after a complicated maneuver involving a key shaped like a long T, a thin flexible pipe.

It was a strange experience, watching that pipe and its attendant

207

wires emerge, foot after foot, from the wellhead, something organic and disturbingly intimate. It reminded me strongly of the aftermath of a sinus operation when the surgeon told me that they needed to remove some gauze packing from the sinus—and he fished inside my nose with forceps and began to pull out an incredible length of bloody gauze strip while my head felt as if it were being unraveled from the inside.

Four hundred feet later, the guys reached the pump, which was shot. "There's your problem," the leader said, squidging up a fingertip's-worth of black muck. I stared at it in horror. It had returned, like the monster in a Fifties sci-fi film. Even the well guy, who knew a thing or two about soils, scowled at it with baffled dislike and started referring to it as "sludge" and "crud." It coated the pipe right from the very top down, he said, and it had made the pump work so much harder that it had burned out in only five years.

He discussed technical remedies while his mate, the one who smoked, picked up the old pump, which looked like a used shell casing, from where they had dropped it in the snow and chucked it into the truck.

I was barely listening, though. My whole sense of the landscape of our house, of solid ground, had been liquefied. Under the house were two tanks, hot and cold, that were now bound to be filled with this black residue, clogging them up, shortening their lives. Under the driveway ran a pipe, also probably sclerotic with black crud, and under them all, four hundred feet under, was this strange dark reservoir, almost incalculably deep, where things flowed and choked and died. I felt like a man who has just had his first heart attack and staggers from the hospital, pamphlets and pictures in hand, knowing that everything he thought he knew about his insides was wrong.

RAMP

After all these years, and even though we both now own Subarus, Barbara still can't stand the driveway. "We need a ramp," she said in the middle of the night.

"A ramp?" I asked, trying to picture this.

What we should do, she said, is enlarge the parking bay at the top so both cars will fit, and then build a ramp, a horizontal walkway from the head of the driveway, entering the house at the second floor—through our bedroom, as things stand.

I mulled this over. Chuck and Helen Vile, next door, have something like this kind of arrangement, but though it would take care of trying to drive up the ridiculous slope, I said, we'd still have to shovel the ramp or salt it or something. I just can't imagine having a whole lot more time or energy to devote to the ramp than we have for the driveway.

The fact is, I told her, probably a third of the homes in Chittenden County have driveways that are as bad as ours right now.

She sighed, and turned over. In the darkness, I could sense her mind extending out into the night outside, moving soil and gravel and even trees into this and then that configuration, trying to make a molehill out of a mountain.

ICE STORM

Last week was disturbingly warm, then we had a quick cold snap and six inches of snow: from my office window at the university I couldn't see the lake or even the town, just gray on white on gray, sketches of gray people leaning into the wind, orange light refracted through driving snow, and the sounds of sirens.

Then the temperature rose a critical few degrees, and the snow moved slowly into a more vertical fall, then turned to rain as Zoë and I were driving home. At first I thought the left-hand wiper must have been bent slightly, because a smeared arc was developing right in front of my face, as inconvenient as possible. Then I thought the heater must not be working. The arc thickened and broadened to take in the entire left-hand edge of the windshield, and by now I was leaning to my right to see out, ducking to look under the mirror. After a while there was no doubt: freezing rain was building up, now not just on the windshield but on the wipers, too, crusts of ice that lifted the wipers off the glass, leaving absurd little cleared curves where the ice itself was doing the wiping.

I told Zoë the story of picking Sally and Colin, Tom and Rose up from the airport in Montreal when they visited, five winters ago, and coming south through freezing rain. At one point I made the mistake of using my windshield washer, and the entire panorama vanished except for a kind of letterbox about five inches wide and two or three inches high above the heater vent, right in front of me but so low I had to drive hunched over. Two or three times I stopped to scrape, but the ice was so thick I could only chip back a little around the letterbox, which began to fill in again as soon as we got moving. I was getting shooting pains through my upper back when we saw the first signs for Burlington—but just as we passed under the Patchen Road bridge, with no more than half a mile to go, the letterbox froze over completely, and I had to slow down and drive along the shoulder, straining to look through a windshield that was as opaque as the window of the lavatory on a train.

Overnight it rained harder, and by morning the snow had that glazed, confectionery look. The list of schools closed or delayed—actually, almost none were delayed—was the longest I'd ever heard, a clean sweep across the region, as if a giant wiper blade had swept across from the Adirondacks, spreading a thick layer of ice. The road was silent.

The girls cheered, Barbara baked muffins, and the house took on the smell of pumpkin. The birch tree by the back deck bowed lower and lower under the weight of ice, each twig and catkin encased in ice as if preserved in a test tube, until the nearer branches were rattling against the house. A couple of the higher branches snapped off entirely. Barbara and then Zoë whacked the tree with a long cardboard tube, hoping to knock off some of the ice and relieve the birch of its weight, but only succeeded in breaking off dozens of twig tips, which tinkled down on the ice-crusted snow on the deck.

It was still raining at ten o'clock when Barbara went out to scrape her car, but by now it was warmer, and the ice slid off her windows in satisfying sheets. She called from the road to say that driving was easy. I took the girls out at 2:30, and by then the driveway was a remarkable layer cake: water on ice on snow on water on ice. Intermittently a gust of wind would stir a tree and send the ice from the topmost branches crashing through the tree, dislodging the lower ice in a white cascade, like the names tumbling down a railway departure board.

Downtown it was a good forty degrees, and almost all the ice had melted or fallen. But the weather was still changing, and when we all drove back out to Essex around 6:30 p.m. after a swim at the Y, the wind had picked up and the trees were doing the stiff, leafless dance of a winter gale. By late evening gusts were rising to fifty miles per hour, and even with the storm windows shut the curtains stirred. The birch, which had now risen more than ten feet back up to its usual height, whipped against the roof.

The next morning was brilliant but frigid. When I went out to collect the mail, the driveway looked like a battlefield. The tire ruts were a dark gray where the standing water had frozen overnight. The white strip between them had frozen around yesterday's footprints, and as I crunched uphill the crust shattered like wineglasses. I picked up one small triangle: it was like a flat silver-white geode, rippling smooth but transparent on top, crystalline white underneath, two separate layers. When I tossed it back down onto the battlement of a frozen boot-mark, it tinkled and skittered, but didn't break.

Crossing to the mailbox, I had to step from one tiny streak of grit to another, for everything else was a series of stripes, between white-gray and ochre, all solid as bedrock and frighteningly slick. A propane truck was coming south down the road, trusting itself to no more than twenty miles an hour, and I crossed ahead of it, imagining for an instant the possibility of slipping and falling, skinning my knee but not otherwise hurting myself, but then finding that, once down, I couldn't get purchase enough to stand up again; and the propane truck driver approaching no faster than a road roller but utterly unable to stop or even steer, staring in horror through his filthy windshield.

Yet that was just an illusion, just a phobia: the road was rough and tactile compared to the driveways running off it. That night we went to a street party at #179, a baronial refit standing perhaps one hundred yards back, and we didn't start slipping and clutching at each other until we were off the road. Driveways are always the worst surface, always the worst.

THE SHEER
FUN OF IT

Six and a half years of living on Chapin Road, and I finally made up my mind to meet Grant Corson, who built the Pixie Houses.

Or the Hippie Houses, they're sometimes called, four houses just north of us, in a row but utterly different, defying rowdom. All made apparently of barnboard, all with tin roofs in odd, steep pitches, as if they were thought up as hippie A-frames evolving into more complex but no less angular geometries, but each with its apexes and angles falling in different directions, like a child's blocks rolled casually down four short, steep driveways, to come to rest and be inhabited exactly as and where they landed. I love these houses: on a road of modified capes and split-level ranches, they manage to be individual without being expensive, eccentric, yet somehow in the Vermont vernacular.

My realtor friend Vince, who knows everyone, introduced me to Grant, and I went over to Weed Road, on the Westford border, to meet him in the last house he built, the tiny, compact one for his own retirement, overlooking the slender Brown's River and its calm, fertile floodplain.

He met me at the door, which led right into the kitchen because he hates hallways and corridors for their waste of space. He was of middle height, stocky, cheerful, with a white beard and white hair worn pretty long for someone of his vintage — an inveterate hippie and troublemaker if ever I saw one. Newly married, too, making a mockery of all this nonsense about retiring and going out to pasture. This is the story of his life, and his houses.

"I was born in New York City and came here to go to UVM in 1951. I was seventeen years old. I was a skier. That was the big attraction for me — to go somewhere I could ski. I just fell in love with Burlington. It's funny: at graduation, all of my classmates were heading out for California or New York. If you stayed here, you couldn't find a job. It was pathetic. To be a college graduate looking for a job commensurate with your education — it was very difficult. Any good jobs were sort of passed down in the family. So I carved out my own niche. I started building houses, started getting involved in real estate. I think at that time Walter Munson, Giles Willey and I were the only real-estate brokers dealing in country real estate. What would you say there is now? A hundred and fifty? Two hundred and fifty? Of course, Giles and Walter were very well established — I was the new kid on the block.

"[In 1951] there were almost no new houses. The biggest shock to my system, coming from the city to Burlington, was the fact that people were more open. If you walked down the streets of New York, you didn't look at anybody, no eye contact, you stayed in a cocoon. People in the city walk as fast as they can with one thing in mind: to get where they're going. Back then, in the early Fifties, you walk along Church Street and these little old ladies that I like to call "bridge ladies," you know, with the gloves and the hat with the little veil coming down about to the end of their nose, they'd say "Good morning, dear!" as they passed by. And it'd scare the heck out of me. I'd think, I don't think I know her. Is that some friend of my mother's? What's she doing up here? Totally off the wall. You walk down Church Street now, it's getting more like New York. People are pretty insulated from each other. You may spot somebody you know and stop to chat, but otherwise. . . . It's sad. Now if you go down to the Price Chopper here you see someone get out of their Ford Explorer, set their alarm, beep beep. This is not the Bronx. Nobody's going to steal your car." He shook his head.

"I graduated from UVM in 1961, because I was in the Army for a couple of years, and I worked for a while, couldn't make up my mind what I wanted my degree to be in. The funny thing is, every spare moment as a child I was trying to build something. We had a lot of vacant land around where we lived, on the edge of the city, and I was always organizing troops of other little boys to go out into the woods and build huts. You know, tree forts. Funny—it never really connected with me that that's what I really wanted to do, was to build. It just didn't seem like an option. [My degree was in] business administration.

"Then my dad wanted a cottage built in the country. He wanted to get out of New York in the summers for a little vacation, so that was my first house. I built him a little house up in Underhill Center.

"He was really fussy. I showed him all kinds of places before he settled on that little piece of land up there on Pleasant Valley Road. He wanted to have a view of Mount Mansfield, he wanted to have a brook—so he got his view, he got his brook, his two or three acres. The house is still there. Like most of my houses, when I built it, it was tiny, and now it's been added on to twice. Which is fine. It gave somebody a window of opportunity to afford a house, and then as their income and their need increased they could add on to it.

"I was in my middle twenties at the time. Here's the funny thing. When I was a kid, growing up, my dad was an amateur woodworker, so I was familiar with the tools, of course, and then every summer and every vacation when I went home I'd work for my buddy's father, who was a building contractor in New York. I had no clue I would end up building houses.

"The nice thing about those early days was that you could find your own direction. I don't know if that's true anymore. There was no building code in Vermont—and I'm still not sure there's a formal building code. There's the electrical and plumbing code, which even back then you had to abide by, but developing real estate—at that time you just walked into the town clerk's office and said, "I want a building permit," told them where, and they gave you one.

"Then finally the state and local government got onto the fact that they'd better oversee it a little better. For example, when I built this house five or six years ago I had to give an engineer thirty-three hundred dollars to say that the pure sand that this house is built on would accept effluent." He snorted in derision.

"The houses just sort of evolved, you know? Let's see—I built two houses in Underhill Center that were similar, and then I broke away from that design. I reasoned that a square house could enclose the most square footage with the least amount of exterior walls. We were coming into the energy crisis thing and people were getting excited about having houses that were economical to heat, and so on. So, a square house. They all came from another house I built in Underhill Flats. I was a lister for the town, too, at the time, so I knew how they figured taxes. People were building a lot of raised ranches then. The first level of that raised ranch was still considered a basement. Then if you had a twelve-twelve pitch on the roof, like a Cape Cod–style house, that was considered a finished attic. So I built a house in Underhill Flats, up on Poker Hill Road, a square little house, the first floor was in the ground like a raised ranch. So there's my finished basement. Then I put a twelve-twelve pitch on the roof, and there's my finished attic. Nothing in between. And I put thumb-latches on the doors, because in the listers' book, those were considered substandard. So when they did the appraisal, it would read, 'Hardware: substandard.' I used divided-light windows: they were considered substandard—they were the old style, not a big picture window. So those were the directions I went. Soft, white-pine boards for the floors: substandard."

"My theory was, not everybody is going to like this house, but I only need one buyer. I don't have a whole subdivision full of 'em, they're not cookie-cutter houses. I only need one buyer. People would come and look, and—I had this same experience with all my houses—a couple would come in the door and their eyes would get all big and wide, and they would ask, 'Has anybody put a deposit on this yet? How much do you want for it?' And just be beside themselves.

"Tin roofs. All these houses had tin roofs. I built two houses side by side, and we were just putting the tin roof on the second one when [the neighbor] came out and said, 'Why don't you come over for some coffee cake?' I said, 'We'll be over as soon as we've finished this side of the roof.' We hadn't even started it yet. She said, 'Oh, it'll all be spoiled by then.' I said, 'You watch and see!'

THE SHEER FUN OF IT

And in thirty minutes we had it finished, and we were having coffee and coffee cake. That's the way tin is: it goes on just like nothing.

"Plus—a tin roof lasts forever. Now, the reason I got that idea was that Marvin Weed, down on the corner here—" he gestured to the intersection of Weed Road and Route 128 "—had a guy walking around on his roof, painting the roof. It had gotten a little rusty. And I said, 'Marvin, uh, how old is that roof on the barn?' And he said, 'Well, I'm seventy-two years old, and that roof was on the barn before I was born.' Now, that was in 1961 or 1962, and now, forty-odd years later, that same tin roof is still on that barn, and it hasn't been painted since then. So I said to myself, well, Jeez, most of the asphalt-shingle roofs are, what, twenty-year roofs—why in the world would anybody choose a twenty-year roof over a hundred-year roof? So that's why I went with tin roofs.

"If you get out of Chittenden County and drive up through a lot of rural Vermont, all these houses have tin roofs on them, and the reason for that is that slate roofs really aren't a lifetime roof. Constant maintenance on a slate roof for most of these old houses. The ice dam builds up on the edge of the roof, it melts, thirty, forty slates come off, and if you don't replace them, of course, you've lost your house."

I hooted with laughter. "So the whole design was based on bringing down the property taxes on the house?"4

He looked pained. "Minimizing the taxes was just a bonus. It was mainly about saving energy. The ground floor being partially submerged into the earth means that it's earth-sheltered, so it's going to be less to heat."

So I changed the subject to those four strange little houses down the road from me. What had possessed him to make that little enclave of eccentricity?

"Why did I build on Chapin Road? There was land for sale. Basically, that's what it amounts to. A guy named Charlie Quatt—those lots along there were known as Quatt's Lots. [He had subdivided the land into ten-acre lots] because of the Act 250 loophole, and of course the lots have two hundred feet of frontage on the road, most of them, but because the lots are angled—the property lines are not perpendicular to the road—the lots are really not that wide. If you measured perpendicular from one sideline to the other it might be a hundred and eighty feet, or something. But it's fine. It's kind of sad, though, isn't it: because of the Act 250 constraints, a lot of the land is now sliced up into these long, skinny lots. Does anybody use their back land? Are there any farmers that take advantage of that land? Course, there are no farmers any more, are there?"

This all sounded very true. Our house is on one of Quatt's lots, and our back land is slowly reverting to wasteland.

"I bought it from Quatt, went to the bank and asked for a construction loan. I did all my business with the Howard Bank—it used to be the Essex Trust Company. It was so simple, it was so beautiful in those days. I would go in, talk to the bank manager—it was Earl Reed, Jr. I would talk to Junior, and he would say, 'What do you want to build?' And I'd say, 'Have you got something I can write on?' He would heave this deep sigh and pull an envelope or something out of the trash, and I'd sketch a little house on it, with the approximate square footage, and say, 'This is what I'm going to build, and I need x number of dollars to do it.' He'd just shake his head and say, 'If the bank examiners ever look at this loan, I'm fired.' He'd say, 'Couldn't you get up a set of blueprints?' I'd say, 'Well, I haven't got the house firmly placed in my mind yet.' So he'd loan me the money, and off we'd go. He was a terrific guy. You could do business on a handshake, just about, in those days."

The first house he built on the Quatt land, he said, was a design he called, whimsically, the "Academy" model. "That's the one with the little tower facing the road?"

This is probably the oddest house of the four. The pitch of the roof rises to a small tower, something between a widow-watch for midgets and a short campanile. I've been in that tower; the stairway up to it is so tight and narrow it could have been designed specifically for kids so their parents couldn't follow them up to this odd crow's nest retreat.

"And I notice that somebody has a window-box up there, and they usually have something planted? So that's got a little steeple on it, like a little academy building."

What the architecture critics call an ironic reference.

"And that was just the sheer fun of it. They just evolved, one from the other. The house up in Underhill Flats has a tower right in the center of the roof. The kids who bought that house, Bev and Bill Frank, still live there, they've made it a lot bigger, but I remember driving by Route 15, and there was one point where you could look up and see the house, and there was a Christmas tree up in the tower. It's just been fun to live in these funny little houses.

"There's another house up on Chapin Road—when we got more into the energy crunch thing, I built one that has a greenhouse that runs across the south wall of the house. [Also put a good steep large pitch to the roof] so that if anyone wanted to put up a bank of solar collectors there, they could. The house faced south. That was another earth-sheltered house. When you walked in the front door you would go down six or seven steps into the main level, or up six or seven steps. It's just two bedrooms, with the bathroom in between, and right across the south wall, just four feet deep but the whole width of the house, was this greenhouse. We built a table in there, and a bench for planting, and all this stuff.

"You can build something like that, but will the owner use it? The guy who bought that house, I came in a month or so after he moved in just to see how he was doing, make sure everything was okay, and he had firewood in the greenhouse, he had his summer tires, boxes of stuff—nothing green! But the beauty of that—my kids and I cross-country skied over to that house and it was, like, twenty below zero. I had set the thermostats—of course, in those days we put in electric heat because it was affordable—I had set the thermostats at fifty-five and I just wanted to see how the house was doing. It was a Sunday afternoon. Beautiful, crystal clear day. Twenty below zero. We took our skis off and went into the house, and I was hit by a heat wave. Looked at the thermostat: fifty-five. But the part of the thermostat that showed what the actual temperature was read seventy-five. Went into the greenhouse, and I had a thermometer there; it said ninety-something. So it did what I had hoped it would do.

"That house has what one of my carpenters referred to as a 'hobbit hole.' You go up into the attic and there's a handmade little wooden door with a piece of stained glass in it, a door from the attic, and you go out into a little thing with a curved roof and a railing that looks out over the valley. As we were framing the house up—that's why I could never give Earl Reed, Jr., a set of blueprints, because as the house was being built, either I or one of my guys would say, 'Look, why don't we do this?' Or, 'If we bring this wall just six inches further this way, it'll make that room so and so.' So we would do it. That's the beauty of being flexible, you know? So as we were framing that house up, we were standing in the attic and looking out across the valley, and we decided we could just partition the attic off and not close that gable-end in, but ... We were going to close it off and frame it in, but we thought, well, just framing it in like this would be okay, but why not cut some rafters on an arc like half a barrel?"

I'd never heard of this hobbit hole. Now I've got to figure out who owns this house, and get them to show me over it.

"The reward? Let me give an analogy. Laying a floor with floor tiles, or laying a floor and making a mosaic. I won't say my houses are," he chuckled, "works of art, but the reward to the builder, as opposed to laying little square tiles all over a whole floor — mindless! Endless! To be able to take what you're doing and be able to have fun with it, like creating a mosaic. A design that's pleasing to the eye. That was the fun of those houses. And each one led to another one. What they're doing with it now, who knows? How well those things hold up, I don't know."

He laughed again, struck by a memory. "I built a house up in Underhill Flats, up on Route 15, way out beyond the village. Picked up twelve acres there, made two six-acre lots out of it. Pure gravel. Beautiful soil. One house we built into the side of the hill, and I had just the outside skin on, no windows on this south-facing wall. My youngest daughter and I went up there right before Christmas, and in four-foot-high letters I painted, 'Faith. Hope. Love.' Something like that. And then put a spotlight in the snow, to shine on it. You know, Christmas season.

"Of course, in those days my beard was down to here, and I

probably had long hair. Somebody driving by saw me up there, doing this, and called the Underhill Town Clerk because they were concerned that a religious cult was moving in!" He chuckled heartily. "I got this call from the clerk. She was hysterical. 'What are you doing now?' she says. I said, 'Well, it's Christmas, for God's sakes! Cut me some slack here! I'm trying to spread good cheer!'

"I look back on it now, and for every one of those houses I was probably the major physical contributor, because my guys would work five days a week and I would go up on weekends quite often. I had the option—I mean, I certainly had the training and background to understand that I could make more money if I drove a Cadillac, wore a suit, smoked a cigar and had three or four crews working for me. I wanted to make a living, but it wasn't about the money. It was about the houses.

"I used to drive my dad crazy, because he would come up for the summer, and he used to want to come over and putter with me, and I'd always get to the end of the driveway, stop the car, get out, turn around and just stand there. He'd always say, 'Come on, I want to get home for supper!'

"I'd say, 'Yeah, okay, we'll get there.' And I just would soak it all in."

He sighed.

GRAVEL PRINCESS

This is a great day. I've managed to find two yards of Shur-Pac without having to go to Hinesburg Sand and Gravel.

Acting on a whim, I went down to the Town of Essex garage, where they directed me cheerfully to John Leo's landscaping/ earthmoving/trucking/excavating/whatever business on Route 15, and though Leo's didn't have proper washed gravel, which apparently is becoming increasingly rare and expensive, they had Shur-Pac, a gravel-soil mix that perfectly matches the color of the existing driveway.

"Depends on what rock they're blaastin' that day," observed Jason, the clerk writing up my order. "Might come out purple. This is from Whitcomb's, over in Colchester."

He walked me round to the back and showed me the second of several piles of different-colored soils like an interior decorator holding up a swatch of wallpaper, or a length of curtain. "That'll do," I said.

Jason climbed into a small member of the bulldozer family called a Case 721 front-loader, dumped my Shur-Pac into a bright-red one-ton truck, and followed me home. The whole delivery took fifteen minutes.

As I stood in the warm, oily air downwind of his truck he engaged the lever and the truck bed rose, and carried on rising. There was that second when it looked as if the stuff would never budge — and then it slid out, pushing up the heavy metal rear gate and landing in a single whoosh I felt through my feet, the flap banging down behind the rush.

That afternoon, I decided, I'd shovel it into the ruts in the driveway, and I'd get Maddy to jump up and down on it with her biggest boots. For the time being, though, she insisted I leave it where it was so she could sit on the pile as if it were a throne, and bury her feet in it.

"I'm the Gravel Princess!" she shouted.

*

Next day, I fill all the spots I missed. I can see them clearly, even though they can be only an inch or so lower, as they're already filled in with leaves. My back ached all last night, feeling not so much strained as dismembered, the components no longer fitting together, and I lay awake listening to the rain and feeling small centipedes of discomfort twist in among my vertebrae.

There's enough Shur-Pac left over for a fresh layer on all the weeds and decomposing ash leaves on the landing at both sides of the head of the driveway, too, and by the time I've finished—well, by the time I'd had enough of throwing wet Shur-Pac, which is almost as heavy as wet snow—the driveway gives the illusion of being not only extended and smoothed but also more proper, in the way that nicely gravelled walks in stately homes are proper. This Shur-Pac is certainly much more rustic and yellow-brown than that clean white aristocratic gravel, but even so it makes the driveway's geometry seem intentional; the smooth curves with which the driveway broadens out to meet the road look like equations plotted on a bucolic graph, imply that the right thing has been done. It looks almost beautiful.

The broader landings give me the absurd feeling that I am now part of a broader world just because the Shur-Pac flows up and out more expansively into the road, or the road now has less impedance, less friction, as it flows into the driveway. I'm reminded of Jason Bankston, a trucker I met in Wyoming, and his motto: "Everything you own came by truck."

Everything in my house came down that driveway. Groceries every day. Friends and family. The moving van that snapped branches off the overhanging sumac and lilac trees. Loads in the back of a Volvo, a Toyota, or a trio of Subarus. I still can't fully believe that a Monitor kerosene heater and a seven-foot metal desk from the university surplus supplies depot both came on the roof of my Volvo. The Monitor wasn't especially heavy, but it was large and full of fuel, and as I inched down the driveway I expected any second that it would tip forward, crash onto the roof, and kerosene would cascade down over the windshield. The desk—how did I do it? I must have had help to flip it over and rope it to the roof, but somehow I got it down by myself without stripping all the paint off the car or slipping half a dozen disks, then turned it over, crawled under the knee-well, straightened up so it rested on my hunched back, and carried it in through the garage, through Zoë's room downstairs, and into my office. Five years later, when it had been in every downstairs room and was now scheduled to leave, I couldn't imagine going through all that again. I went at it with a screwdriver and a hacksaw, and it made its final journey up the driveway in pieces.

And this is when it strikes me, to my astonishment, that I have now lived in this house longer than I've lived anywhere else in my life.

That's enough shoveling for now. Holding the spade, I trudge down the driveway, and on comes the motion-detector light I installed, thinking it would scare away the deer from the vegetable garden. As far as I know it never did, and over time three of its four bulbs have burned out, but every time I come home late, tired, perhaps cold, carrying my pack and probably an armful of other junk as well, perhaps treading gingerly down the packed snow and ice, perhaps with Zoë, who is still a little afraid of the darkness of the country road at night—every time, when I'm halfway down the driveway, that light comes on.

Tim Brookes was born in England and worked as a singer, songwriter, guitarist, and tour guide before moving to Vermont. He is the author of *Catching My Breath*, *Signs of Life*, and *A Hell of a Place to Lose a Cow*, which was selected as one of the top travel books of the year by *The New York Times* and *Booklist*. Many of the essays in *The Driveway Diaries: A Dirt Road Almanac* were aired on National Public Radio.

Printed in the United States
137397LV00002B/234/A